KEEPING THE FAITH

THE BATTLE FOR AUSTRALIAN CATHOLICISM

JAMES GRANT

CONNOR COURT PUBLISHING

Published in 2017 by Connor Court Publishing Pty Ltd

Copyright © James Grant

All rights reserved. No part of this book may be reproduced or transmitted in any form or by any means, electronic or mechanical, including photocopying, recording or by any information storage and retrieval system, without prior permission in writing from the publisher.

Connor Court Publishing Pty Ltd
PO Box 7257
Redland Bay QLD 4165

sales@connorcourt.com
www.connorcourtpublishing.com.au
Phone 0497 900 685

ISBN: 9781925501704

Front Cover Design: Maria Giordano

Front Cover photo taken by Francesca Golotta, used with permission

Printed in Australia

Special thanks to my wife Dolores, Richard Alston and Bishop David
Robarts for their ongoing support and encouragement

In grateful remembrance of Peter Keating

*"Freedom consists not in doing what we like,
but in having the courage to do what we ought"*
(Pope John Paul II, 1995)

ABOUT THE AUTHOR

Fr James Grant MAICD BA BTh GDip IS GDip Comp ST GDip Trauma Counselling.

Born in Adelaide, and schooled in Essendon, Victoria. Fr James joined the Commonwealth Police in 1977 with an initial posting in Canberra. He has qualified as a martial arts instructor in Brazilian Jiu Jitsu, scuba diving and played first grade cricket for Northcote.

Fr James undertook theological studies at Melbourne University, graduating in 1984. Appointed to the UK as an associate priest, He became one of London's first white vicars to minister to the expanding West Indian community Fr James initiated his first interfaith gatherings in west London following the Brixton riots, after which he was appointed on short term placement to Berlin (west Germany) in 1988 and Budapest in 1989.

Fr James returned to Australia in 1989 where he was Senior Chaplain at Geelong Grammar School for seven years, followed by two years at St Michael's grammar and six years at The Peninsula School. He was noted for his pastoral care with a focus on martial arts, football and cricket as methods for building confidence in students.

In 2004 he was appointed a parish priest at St Stephen's Richmond, then in 2005 Melbourne's first team vicar for the new parish of Jika Jika in Melbourne's north with responsibility for a large Sudanese refugee community. As Parish priest for the Preston area, he was a strong advocate for the Nuba people, of Sudan, who are experiencing genocide. He has built two schools in Northern India.

Fr James founded Chaplains Without Borders in 2004 to initiate new ventures into corporate and community organisations, and CWB grew to be Australia's largest chaplaincy service within 2 years. He went on to be appointed as the world's first chaplain to the casino industry in 2006 (Crown Enterprises Australia) a position he still retains.

As a leading traditionalist within the Australian church, Fr James supported the development to the Anglican Ordinariate in Australia and served on the national committee as secretary 2010-2011. Fr James was received into the Catholic Church and ordained as a Catholic Priest in September 2012 as a foundational priest for the Australian Ordinariate. In 2012 he was appointed National director for Ordinariate schools and to the Ordinariate governing council.

Fr James has continued to develop missions including Catholics in Business 2012 and Catholics in Mission and renewal in 2013. His CYA (Catholic Youth Academy) youth program works through Crown casino to develop confidence in de-motivated young Australians and find work placements within Crown. In 2013 he co-established the Renewal Centre.

He is the first Chaplain appointed to an A league soccer club in Australia at the largest Australian club, Melbourne Victory. He is involved with 9MM and 45ACP pistol competition and is completing PPL training for Helicopters.

In 2015 Fr James established the Father James Grant foundation, implementing programs for de-motivated young Australians. The "mission Engage" program has now helped around 100 young Australians find their first Job. The Resurgence Group is a team designed to help parishes re-energize their community life.

      www.chaplainswithoutborders.org
      www.catholicsinbusiness.org
      www.thefatherjamesgrantfoundation.org
      www.resurgence.org.au

FOREWORD

Father James Grant is a positive person and his latest work, *Keeping the Faith* is an incredibly optimistic book. It is precisely the sort of book that is required for these difficult times. It's a clear-eyed assessment of the very major challenges faced not just by the Catholic Church in Australia, but which confront our entire society. But the central purpose of the book is not to provide a catalogue of ills. Crucially, Fr James provides a way forward for the Catholic Church. He charts a course for how the Church can continue to make the sort of contribution to Australian society that it has in the past and which has helped make this country the safe, secure, and prosperous country that it is.

Fr James is absolutely correct when he writes that the Catholic Church must rediscover its purpose. It is a purpose that is not to simply repeat and amplify whatever happens to be the popular progressive cause of the day. As Fr James explains 'popularity' and 'relevance' are fleeting. Whether for individuals or institutions the search for popularity requires constant change. Whether a cause is popular says nothing about whether it is important. It is dangerous for the Church to pursue popular causes that are antithetical to what the Church stands for. Throughout history the most vital role of the Church has been to stand against what's been wrong, but nevertheless popular. The Church should not pander to a popularity confected by the media than it should ally itself to the government of the day. And of course to point out this truth about popularity is to risk being unpopular. When popular causes centre on 'Identity Politics' the Church should be especially wary of courting popularity. 'Identity Politics', which in broad terms seeks to categorise individuals not according to their status as individuals but as merely part of a group identified by their class, race, or gender is a notion that is hostile to every one of the Church's teaching. The very basis of Christianity is that we are all equal in God and of equal moral worth regardless of our skin colour or anything else. Identity Politics denies the individuality that God has endowed us all with. According to Identity Politics we are to receive praise or blame because of what others who are part of identity group have done or not done. According to Identity Politics decisions that individuals make are not the result of choices, or their virtue or their evil, they are simply the product of their identity – an identity over which they have no influence.

An illustration of the wholly negative impact of the ideology of identity politics is provided by Fr James when he talks about the tragedy of St James Church in Brighton, Melbourne. The 123-year-old church was destroyed by a fire in 2015, the cause of which has never been discovered. On the day of the church's destruction, the actor Rachel Griffiths said 'I was quite elated, like many of my generation when I heard the news this morning. It's always been a difficult building for us to drive past because there's been so much tragedy and complicated feelings, I guess.' Griffiths was referring to the fact that a criminal had been previously been the church's parish priest. Griffiths comment that she was elated a church had burnt down passed largely without comment, which of itself reveals a great deal about the current status of Christianity in Australia. If such a remark had been made about the destruction of a place of worship of another religion it's doubtful whether it would have been greeted with the shrugging of shoulders. But there's something more than this. Griffiths betrayed the kind of thinking that underlies identity politics. According to her the current parishioners of St James Church should suffer for the criminal actions of an individual that occurred twenty-five years ago. Instead of holding individuals responsible for their actions, groups of people, in this case the members of the parish must be forced to bear collective guilt.

Keeping the Faith is more than simply an important and timely book. It's a work that's absolutely necessary. I have no doubt that Fr James' clear-eyed assessment of the challenges the Catholic Church faces, and his courage in declaring what needs to be done will give heart to the very many people of faith who feel exactly the same as he does. The Catholic Church in Australia needs many more Fr James's. It needs people of goodwill and of a good heart who are willing to stand up for what they believe and who are not afraid to stand up for the mission of the Church.

-- John Roskam, Executive Director, Institute of Public Affairs.

PREFACE

That there is a significant challenge to the way the world has been run probably since the Enlightenment is now generally accepted, and its manifestation has been particularly noticeable over the last few decades. The challenge comes both from internal and external sources. It can be a contest of ideas but it can also be a contest of force using violence. It can be between individuals or groups within our Liberal Democracies magnified by a media which has an agenda, but it can also be a threat to change nations by force as state on state violence or through terrorist groups. The birth place of our Judeo Christian culture, the Middle East, has seen all of these tendencies come to the fore, and generations have been destroyed.

The liberal democracies, often referred generally as The West, face a particular threat because we pride ourselves on the openness of our societies. Those that oppose us, will exploit that openness. The choice that we face in the West and particularly in Australia, is the compromise that so often needs to be made between our freedoms and our security.

Often the most dangerous threat to what we are and what we should be, and the limits of change that we can tolerate are more insidious than obvious. All societies change but there must be value in change. Too often, the most generous interpretation of those who make the most noise are advocating change for change sake.

The Church and its leaders are critical in leading society through the process of establishing what change is good and what is detrimental. But at a time when we as a society should be able to turn to our church leaders for philosophical advice on what has been tried many times before and found to fail, the church has lost its occupation of the moral high ground, and the churches good leaders are not being listened to, and many are not talking sense.

Keeping the Faith puts forward a basic theory in the first seven short chapters that the church has become fearful of criticism and is no longer promoting the things it alleges it stands for. Father James makes the case that the adoption of many socialist ideas especially in the social justice framework, is a poor attempt to be popular and has not delivered any increase in Mass attendance. My impression of such attempts are that they are amateurish because our Church leaders are not experts in this field, and many people are sick of "Lefty" solutions for aboriginals, refugees and climate change.

Additionally, the cradle of our culture, the schools, are deeply confused, sometimes teaching more Dreamtime than Catholicism. Some schools are more about producing activists and have even ignore Western civilisation. Finally the church, having lost the public space, does not resist those who would seek to push it out and keep it out – mainly Green and socialists of many types.

In the next 13 short chapters, Father James offer solutions, such as promoting Western civilisation, opposing the nanny state, defending free markets, contesting calls for sharia law, standing up for persecuted Christians. If we don't know what is valuable in our society, how will we ever know where to draw the line.

Of particular interest, Father James focuses on a successful model – Poland under the Nazis and Communists, and look at how they managed to keep their culture and faith. Indeed, we have a lot to learn. The book concludes by looking at a way of getting the church and its leaders, and its beliefs, back into the public space by creating and supporting work initiatives for young Australians. To me, Father James is talking Catholicism 101 but we no longer do any of it. This book, its identification of the problem and offering of solutions, is a strong call to get moving and create another narrative other than clergy abuse.

I believe that for all the faults of Australian society, we are the epitome of development of The West. As a privileged member of this society, my rights are more protected here than anywhere else in the world. For those less fortunate than I, the chance of doing well in this society, of bettering ourselves by honest effort and strong values, is greater in Australian society than anywhere else in the world.

Western Culture has been challenged many times over the last 2000 years. It has bent, in some places it has broken and where it has broken, it has mended itself and become better. Australians should have confidence that we and our values can survive, but we must fall not fall asleep at the wheel.

The church must be there leading, not in giving away rights and values to be popular, but in knowing where change can occur, because the church and its leaders more than anyone else, should know what is worth defending in our society.

Jim Molan *AO DSC former Senior Officer in the Australian Army And Commander of the multi-national task force in Iraq in 2004.*

CONTENTS

Introduction: The Hard Truth for Catholicism   17

What's gone wrong?

I   A Church in fear   21

II   False economics and reliance on government   30

III   Social justice chaos   37

IV   Theology that erodes   51

V   School confusion   57

VI   Loss of the public space   64

VII   Our current idea of welfare harms Catholicism   73

Solutions

VIII   Successful example: Poland   80

IX   Reclaiming a Voice: Returning to the public square   90

X   Affirm and promote freedom of speech   96

XI   Affirm Western civilisation   104

XII   Oppose the Nanny State   117

XIII   Defending the free market   124

XIV   Make a genuine difference to the poor   130

XV   Contesting Sharia Law   136

XVI Reclaim the workplace   146

XVII Stand up for persecuted Christians   154

XVIII What to do about Robots   161

XIX Be yourself: Contending with a bio-enhanced society   167

XX The Catholic case for lower taxes with Aaron Lane   172

INTRODUCTION

THE HARD TRUTH FOR CATHOLICISM

Australia is in the midst of significant cultural change. The rise of radical individualism has seen many of the institutions and community services, such as police, teachers and politicians losing community respect and viability, to the point where many of them function at significantly reduced capacity.

The Australian Catholic Church has been the last domino to fall. The depth of depravity in clergy sexual abuse has dramatically dismantled community trust in both clergy and the wider teachings of the Church. This disintegration is set to continue for many decades to come. We now see in Australia, a Catholic Church, apprehensive and timid in its relationship to wider Australia and largely ineffective in combatting the forces of cultural decline. Indeed, the Australian Catholic Church has no effective voice or mechanism for presenting any of its values, purposes, teachings or hope to the wider Australian Community: The Catholic Church in Australia is now reduced to the same level of impact as any community club or association, with most Australians expecting it to behave in like manner to a bowling or rotary club. Do some good local things, but do not attempt to project your values or beliefs in the public realm.

This is not a book specifically about why things have come to this state, but a call for Catholic recognition of the true state of affairs and a proposal for repairing a Catholic vitality and voice in Australian community life.

The visible decline in Western Catholicism in Europe, Ireland and Australia has been alarmingly sudden. Indeed, this disintegration has taken place in the course of one average Australian lifespan. The current circumstances see young European and Australians not just rejecting Catholicism, but having no experience of it in the first place. The vast majority of under 40's are entirely ignorant of the teachings and practices of the historical Catholic faith.

I am not a priest who subscribes to a diminished Catholic future, nevertheless Catholics must be very clear about how to remain as a vital, engaged force for change and betterment in the lives of individual Australians and our wider community.

I do not advocate the path undertaken by Australia's protestant churches, who have subordinated so much of Christian teaching to secular values. Sadly, their faith is now devoid of power and life. A Christianity which suggests the highest goods are to be happy in life, feel good about yourself and be fair to others is devoid of life and not the path Catholicism should be taking. Unfortunately there are many concerning signs that some Catholics see this cul-de-sac as a way forward. I am advocating another future, one that acknowledges that Catholics must bring clear and positive, yet relevant views to the table. We cannot continue with business as usual.

Australian Catholics can no longer focus on the same old social justice issues, in which we are not experts, have modest financial commitment and do not impact mainstream Australia. A message of refugees, indigenous issues and climate change brings us no credit and is not frankly our "core" business.

The fundamental Catholic concern has always been for the health of the individual and, by natural extension, the health of the family.

Therefore, it is imperative that we bring something fresh to the contemporary environment. It can no longer be what can Catholics do for their church, but what is their church offering? Many Catholics hunger for something more than material prosperity.

In my view, this means no longer talking about increased handouts and financial transfers, but action in the world of work.

To strengthen and contribute to the world of work is the great Catholic good in the West. Work is the basis of self-esteem, the foundation for marriage, the security of house and children, and the protection on which parish community life is built. A Catholic church again focused on the world of work, advocating for the dignity of the human person in work, developing and expanding employment, training and supporting the young towards gaining and maintaining their first job. Then we really would be bringing something precious to the Australian community. Before we can meaningfully debate the future of work, we need a clear eyed understanding of the market economy with its benefits and shortcomings rather than a relentless and selective negativity leading to evermore government handouts.

The time for fear is over, we must begin again, but we must also speak clearly about what we believe and who we are. We have been devalued and oppressed before. In the first century the church survived and grew, despite extensive persecution. We have defeated the tyranny of Nero, Caligula, Domitian, Stalin and Hitler. Now is the time to begin again as a viable alternative to a society of depression, hopelessness and self-indulgence.

I

A CHURCH IN FEAR

In March 2015, St James, Brighton was burnt to the ground in a fire police treated as suspicious. The parish was a viable community of around 350 parishioners, with a heritage listed building of immense historical importance and one of Melbourne's most popular venues for weddings. Yet like many Australian parishes it had suffered at the hands of a nefarious paedophile priest for a period of eight years in the 1980's and early 1990's. Yet perhaps more shocking than a deliberately lit fire was the comments of one particular local celebrity and the insipid response of the Melbourne Archdiocese.

Within two hours of the commencement of the fire which took five hours to control, the Australian actress Rachel Griffiths had gone on Melbourne ABC radio to say "I was quite elated when I heard the news this morning. It's always been a difficult building for us to drive past, because there's been so much tragedy and complicated feelings. We've attended many funerals of boys we now know were abused by that priest ... at the actual Church that it occurred in."

To these supercharged emotional comments, the Melbourne Archdiocese had no response. For those of us gathered that evening to view their destroyed parish the lack of a bishop to witness and console the Parish family was noted and not inconsiderably added to the beginnings of an awareness. "Why is nobody from the Church here? It feels like we are abandoned."

As events unfolded, it would indeed be the case that this parish was abandoned but that painful gathering was to highlight and to reinforce a significant failing of the Australian Church; yes Melbourne is a large diocese, yet, when significant and tragic events occur, bishops must be seen with their people. When this fails to happen for months and months after event, local people quickly pick up a strong message; we don't matter!

The tragedy of St James almost immediately became "an issue" in that it highlighted the Archdiocese's inability to care for each part of its organisation. The indifference to the needs of these parishioners, who had just lost their Church, was extremely poor. They needed to be told they mattered, they needed to hear that when a parish is physically and verbally attacked, the Church will defend them. They needed to hear of death and resurrection, what they got was a black hole of nothingness!

In a society which no longer has a natural affinity with religion or Catholicism, Catholic communities must be quickly supported and defended. If we do not do this we erode our communities. We must acknowledge that we are under attack from the forces of secularisation that are equally as destructive to the Church as communism and fascism were. Our current "do nothing" attitude is a key factor in Australian Catholic decline. If St James Brighton, which includes 350 faithful Catholics will not be defended, what will be? Herein lies a key component in Catholic destruction, ironically from within.

There is no doubt that St James Brighton had come to be seen by many as the "poisoned chalice of the diocese". Not ironically from the damage done by a paedophile priest but from the local battles between the parish and the school, in a classical division between left-green leaning school parents and principal and a conservative clergy and parish base. The reality of a paedophile clergyman could be easily constructed into a paradigm that suggested that traditional clergy, liturgy and devotion to Mary was intimately linked to paedophile clergy. The failure of St James Church to embrace a left-green ideology of refugees, indigenous issues and climate change could only mean the Church was seen by progressive parents as irrelevant and not a place that was suitable for their children. The behaviour of this former priest, deeply depraved and corrupt was quickly commandeered to portray the church as old, irrelevant, out of touch and part of something called "Old Catholicism" which must never be revisited. The fact that St James was the only church in the region with a significant devotion to Our Lady, was not seen as worthy of retention.

The merging with an adjoining parish in 2016 and the appointment of a radical liberal priest would significantly hasten the sense of abandonment experienced by St James parishioners.

Without doubt something is happening to Australian Catholicism. The Church, is now seen to be afraid, timid and with a desperate desire to be accepted by wider Australia, especially those elements that seek to promote, multi-culturalism, socialism, refugees and indigenous advancement. The Australian Catholic Church has now entered a domain where the promotion or sustaining of Catholic communities is not possible if it comes against a prevailing societal view. St James, Brighton, is a bleak case in point.

The Catholic Church now appeases those who remind them of clergy abuse or any groups that negatively bring to mind Catholic culture, beliefs or independence. These groups espouse that Catholicism is not unique, has no inherent claim to truth and may only participate in Australian society if it is compliant with their view of mainstream values. The leadership of the Church seems unable to summon sufficient pride, resilience or unity to ensure appeasement does not continue to take place. Unfortunately in failing to confront these challenges the fears for the Catholic Church are quickly coming to fruition – loss of a public voice, drastic decline in numbers and internal collapse.

The Catholic Adoption of Socialism as a Modus Operandi

Marxist and socialist ideas have brought death, trauma and dislocation to many part of the world and continue to plague the modern world, particularly in Venezuela, North Korea, Cuba, Vietnam, China and Bolivia.

Regrettably, the Australian Catholic Church has adopted

a substantial number of socialist ideas in a frantic attempt to maintain relevance within mainstream Australia. In this transition Catholicism has echoed the path taken 20 years earlier by the Australian Protestant churches many who now support marriage equality, radical women's reproductive rights and transgender positions, yet have still quickly slipped into irrelevance. The Catholic Church faces the same irrelevance in its sharing of a large number of core socialist positions. Some of these include increased taxation, greater welfare transfers, criticisms of global trade agreements, extreme indigenous rights and environmentalism. Whilst the Catholic Church is also fundamentally a supporter of social equality and egalitarianism, its language and policy advocacy strongly reflect left wing political movements.

This Catholic confusion is manifest even within the Vatican and the thinking of Pope Francis. Unquestionably, Pope Francis has rejected some Marxist philosophy and analysis, and has canonised some Catholics martyred by communist regimes. Yet he also seems to commend and equate communism, socialism and Christianity for their work and support with the poor. In a 2016 interview with the Marxist journalist Eugenio Scalfari which focused on equality, rights and greater freedoms the Pope was asked.

> ES – "So you yearn for a society where equality dominates. This as you know is the program of Marxist socialism and of communism. Are you therefore thinking of a Marxist type of society?"
>
> Francis – "It has been said many times and my response has always been that if anything it is the communists who think like the Christian. Christ spoke of a society where the poor, the weak and the marginalised have the right to decide. Not demagogues, not

Barabbas, but the poor, whether they have faith in a transcent God or not. It is they who must help to achieve equality and freedom."

This thinking is at the core of the problem facing the Australian Church. To suggest that communists think like Christians shows no understanding of either world history, lived experience or Christian theology. For the Church to no longer understand the differences between its founder's teachings and the ravages inflicted on humanity by communism and socialism is astonishing and bewildering.

Communism and socialism are grounded in atheism with a central emphasis on materialism. Christ's teaching rejected both such intellectual positions. In history all of the world's significant socialists from Engels, Marx, Stalin, Mao through to Morales, Chavez or the Australian Socialist Alliance, all end up with philosophical versions of the end justifies the means. Hence, the experience of socialism is always one concerned with crushing oppositions, extreme attacks on the individual, coercion and dictatorship.

The current Australian Catholic perspective which sometimes involves and couples the faith in traditional socialistic agendas, actually treats the poor not as human beings who need to be loved and assisted but in a materialist and instrumental way, which sees those in poverty as being without skills, beliefs or ideas needing only to be funded in sufficient ways to change their economic status. Such an exclusive economic focus ignores the great Christian teaching that poverty resides within the mind and the soul. For

Christians it is not only those who may be unemployed who are poor but those who are self-focused, lack the will to contribute or who cannot see value in family, children, the unborn, or a society focused on attitudes of love, value and respect.

This form of poverty, which is at the root of all poverty, has nothing to do with welfare provision or economic security. At the moment Australian Catholics never speak of or challenge this form of poverty.

In Christian terms this form of poverty should be self-evident to Pope Francis having lived alongside Argentina's own Marxist movement the 'Ejercito Revolucionario Del Pueblo', who had no hesitation engaging in kidnapping and assassination in an effort to overthrow government and establish a dictatorship of the proletariat.

Pope Francis has focused heavily in his pontificate on issues of inequality; indeed he sees this as one of the key dilemmas facing the Church and the modern world. Yet, primarily this attention to inequality is centrally focused only on economic inequality.

> "What we want is a battle against inequality, this is the greatest evil that exists in the world. It is money that creates it and that goes against those measures that try to make wealth more wide spread and thus promote equality" (Pope Francis, Scalfari interview).

Nevertheless an exclusive socialist-like emphasis on economic inequalities fails to note that dictatorial and socialist regimes, such as Sudan, North Korea, Cuba, Bolivia and Venezuela are the primary cause of poverty throughout the world. It is not lack of money that affects these nations but the stupidity of corrupt and perverse spending which ironically benefits the socialist elite but does nothing for the poor.

In Western nations poverty is clearly witnessed in the self-absorption which continues to terminate unborn children with little discussion beyond a rights agenda. The long term impact on mothers, fathers and society beyond a women's right to choose is no longer important. In the Islamic world the savage application of Sharia law in both Sunni and Shia communities sees women unable to study overseas, unable to participate in most activities or obtain an individual passport without male permission. Under Sharia law a women inherits generally half that of a man, "Allah enjoins you concerning your children: the male shall have the equal of the portion of two females (Koran 4,11-12) a man may divorce his wife unilaterally through "talaq" whereas woman are limited to divorce only under specific and rare circumstances such as male impotence.

These are all examples of the profound poverty found throughout the world. The current Catholic focus on only a narrow economic definition of poverty leaves the Church's mission in the world severely diminished. When we consider what should be the fullness of the Catholic response to poverty, we can unfortunately see a narrowing of poverty to single issues dictated by concepts like economic inequality. The poverty of Western social distress sees high divorce rates, excessive dependence on the State, unemployment, under-valued children, abortion, overwhelmed police, teaching and medical professions. When we couple this with political cultures besotted with climate change, rights without responsibilities, and no concern for cultural identity and then add the problems of division and injustice brought by Sharia law, it is easy to see that the Catholic Church is currently not capable of speaking to modern Australia, let along offering valuable or useful insights. The fear which has infected Catholic leadership, its agencies and its local parishes is hastening the rapid slide to irrelevance.

II

FALSE ECONOMICS AND RELIANCE ON GOVERNMENT

Pope John Paul II has rightly been acclaimed as the pre-eminent Catholic thinker on questions of the economy and its role within the life of the Church, society and government.

Whilst John Paul II was sensibly cautious in advocating for the economic structure of any particular nation, he was also intensely categorical in condemning the systems and practices within economics that are life-crushing and inimical to the spirit of Catholicism. The Pope's economic thinking was heavily centred in apostolic Catholic traditions, namely that human life is grounded in a divine dignity, that humanity must be free to work and create as part of the divine calling and that the key economic role of the State must be to protect such God given freedoms.

This grounding in Catholic thought led to a number of strong assertions in economic philosophy that John Paul II recognised as essential in upholding the dignity and work of humanity in economic life.

John Paul II was a ferocious critic of socialism and worked all his life to bring about its destruction in his native Poland and wider Eastern Europe: "The historical experience of socialist countries has sadly demonstrated that collectivism does not do away with alienation, but rather increases it, adding to it, a lack of basic necessities and economic inefficiency" and "The fundamental error of socialism is anthropological in nature ... the good of the individual is completely subordinated to the functioning of the socio-economic mechanism ... the concept of the person as an autonomous subject of moral decision disappears ... a person who is deprived of something he can call his own, and the possibility of earning a living through his own initiative, comes to depend on the social machine and on those who control it. This makes it much more difficult for him to recognise his dignity as a person, and hinders progress towards the building up of an authentic human community".

John Paul II witnessed first-hand the corrosive nature of socialism, both in the effects on individuals and society, but also its antagonistic hostility to the community of faith. Nevertheless, John Paul II also noted the life-destroying nature of the Western secular state whose ethos is prevalent throughout all levels of Australian Government. In his encyclical *Centesimus Annus* (1991) and speaking of Pope Leo, he notes "on the contrary, he frequently insists on necessary limits to the State's intervention and on its instrumental character, inasmuch as the individual, the family and society are prior to the State, and inasmuch as the State exists in order to protect their rights and not to stifle them".

Recent developments in the State of Victoria would suggest an invasive control being applied to the freedom of both individuals and the Catholic Church. In December 2015 in an attempt to further secularise public schools, the socialist state government issued a new directive restricting the way teachers talk about religious ideas in our schools. The most disturbing aspect of the new government approach is that the teaching and singing of traditional Christmas carols will now be banned. The State Government notes that it is not banning all carols, just those that refer to God! It is not difficult to see that the underlying attack is not really directed at Christmas carols, but is a wider attempt to strip away the meaning of Christmas. Such attacks on Christian culture are typical of the action of previous socialist governments in Poland and Eastern Europe. They do nothing to protect the rights of individuals and families, prescribing even what is able to be sung.

Additionally, Victoria has funded the radical so called Safe Schools Coalition, which has been established to develop anti-bullying programs specifically for same sex attracted and transgender children. The Safe Schools Coalition also received $8m in Federal funding, notwithstanding the fact that bullying directed towards this group of children represented less than 1% of all bullying cases.

The Safe Schools Coalition has a number of radical agendas specially designed to promote awareness of homosexual and transsexual issues. It promotes gender theories that are not scientifically supported and encourages political activism strongly advocating for students and teachers to participate in political marches and demonstrations.

Its affiliate website "minus 18" endorses the viewpoint that gender binary sexuality (male and female) is not real and that bisexuality (attraction to male and female) and transsexuality (attracted to all genders) are valid forms of sexual identity. The covert Safe Schools Coalition agenda is aimed at convincing government teachers, students and parents that homophobic bullying in schools is substantial and should be lessened by promoting transgender and homosexual lifestyles and sexual practices. The Victorian Government is committed to ensuring the program is in all State Secondary Schools by 2019. Here again is another example of an Australian government advocating social positions fundamentally antagonistic to Catholic teaching and practice with barely a word of serious Church criticism.

John Paul II was also very principled in noting that human freedom in economics must be expressed in a manner consistent with virtue and in accord with the common good. Whilst success in business, making money and expressing human freedom in economic activity is a fundamental economic benefit of free markets, this freedom must also be used in a responsible and faith-minded manner.

John Paul II brought to these economic questions a radical new understanding of freedom when he advocated "the right of economic initiative". John Paul II knew from experience that companies compelled by legislation, red tape or government intervention to regulate workforce size, production rates or assigned market outcomes, limit the freedom of enterprise and eventually erode future growth prospects. John Paul II understood that limiting the economic initiative of companies in planning their own future, in taking their own risks and in competing in their own style, ultimately erodes the spirit of initiatives. He rightly concluded that socialistic forms of business which sought to ensure "equality of outcomes" were ultimately guaranteed to fail, because morally they denied the freedom and right of business entrepreneurs. State owned businesses fulfilling State contracts, may ensure initial high employment, but in the end are destined to collapse as they deny human freedom and creativity in its most basic sense.

The teachings of John Paul II strongly affirm that Catholicism has a fundamental interest in the modern business economy. Alongside other human endeavours it is called to advocate for principles of economic freedom and justice directed both for individuals and societies towards the common good.

Australians are continually encouraged to have a strong dependency and attachment to government. Whilst we are happy to admit that we are over governed and that we have too many layers of government, there is no doubt that in times of trouble, violence or even minor disruptions the call will be loudly proclaimed.

> "The Government should do something about this ... the Government needs to change the laws ... the Government should insist on harsher penalties".

In our political life, and among our parliamentary representatives and our political commentators almost all argument within modern Australia is devoted to the failures of government, the need for government to do better and the inability of disconnected or indifferent politicians to listen and relate to the Australian public.

Nevertheless, in recent years Australians have acquired the greatest increase in laws, regulations and workplace rules in our history, despite latent hostility to politicians and government.

Indeed, as Prime Minister, Julia Gillard determined the success of her government by reference to the number of legislative initiatives passed by the Parliament! Unfortunately, much of this legislation was focused on gesture politics and did little to address critical economic realities such as falling productivity growth, increasing employment and sustaining a wider based economic prosperity.

In my view, the key framework for achieving long term economic success is the classic liberal approach, which focuses on maintaining the rule of law, limiting government, protecting private property and cutting red tape.

The Catholic Church in the last thirty years has shown little inclination to support any of these fundamental ideas. In fact, in many areas it has grown hostile to the idea that free markets provide incentives for innovation and the discovery of new economic paths or that such economic interaction ensures that new prosperity meets human needs.

Indeed, political activity from Catholic organisations and

leaders has produced incessant calls for the growth of government, consequently stifling entrepreneurship and shifting the burden of debt onto younger Australians and future generations. Moreover, the Church has also facilitated a disproportionate view of government which sees the State as unchecked in its responsibilities. This unbridled state even suggests that individual wealth is a product of government laws and regulations and that individuals with wealth have in consequence benefitted from a generous government system. Ever increasing economic transfers from individuals to the State is now virtually an unchallenged philosophy. This philosophy now pervades most Australian Catholic aid agencies.

Catholic aid agencies are now fully aligned with the great American champion of this philosophy, former President Barack Obama: "if you were successful somebody else gave you help, somebody helped to create this unbelievable American system that we have allowed to thrive. If you've got a business, you didn't build that, somebody else made that happen". Such a view, now shared by many Catholic agencies attributes all wealth to the State, the State therefore has claims against such wealth. Welfare transfers are but another outcome that suggests private individuals have no real claim over their own wealth.

Pope John Paul II has highlighted the centrality of freedom in economics, and the inability of socialist government to provide for the common good. A Catholic Church which increasingly advocates for governments to resolve welfare, employment and social issues is failing both to understand the proper role of the State and the priority of the individual within it.

III

SOCIAL JUSTICE CHAOS

It has long been obvious that the political agenda of some Catholic organisations and schools rest solidly within the Green-left advocacy model, particularly in its increasing reliance on identity politics. Noel Pearson has rightly highlighted the soft bigotry of many of these groups when he notes "they need blacks to remain alienated from mothers bosoms, incarcerated in legion, leading short lives of grief and tribulation – because if it were not so against whom would they direct their soft bigotry of low expectations" (*The Australian*, November 2016).

The St Vincent de Paul Society has also been drawn sharply to the left of politics under its CEO John Falzon. The perpetuation of low expectations for indigenous Australians is clearly evident in his opinions.

> "There is a deep wound in Australia, it is a wound that is known by different names, colonisation, dispossession, coercion, control. It is still with us ... the policies that the government enshrines as legislation are policies built on the falsehood that the wound does not exist ... they are policies that continue to harm, to hurt, to humiliate, to degrade, to punish, to control, like all forms of colonisation, they deny the full humanity of those who are subject to them" (*The Record*, Spring 2016).

This negative view of indigenous Australians as oppressed and continually held captive by colonial masters is a viewpoint that allows for little creativity or future solutions. Here is just another organisation that in personal terms, encourages "low expectations", indeed this play on alleged oppression can encourage no expectations, apart from ever-more taxpayer funded entitlements.

Marcia Langton, foundation Chair for Indigenous Studies at the University of Melbourne could well be talking directly about the attitudes of the St Vincent de Paul Society:

> "Aboriginal leaders face the very difficult problem of trying to shift recalcitrant people from welfare to work. What solutions do the Greens and inner-city progressives have, apart from arrogantly and heartlessly accusing these leaders of being "Assimilationists". The simple answer is none" (*The Monthly*, May 2015).

It really is time that some Catholic organisations moved beyond the politics of "identity". A worldview that regards some groups as belonging within an oppressed category and others as belonging to the evil oppressors only encourages demands for more help and entitlements from the Government" and enshrines permanent failure. Fortunately, many indigenous Australians and refugees advocates now realise the perversity of those secretly ensuring failure through the creation of victims and the bigotry of low expectations.

The Catholic Church is currently in permanent crisis, the results of clergy abuse scandals and the ill-advised uptake of leftist causes in many of its agencies and schools. Death by a thousand cuts awaits unless the Church can again speak to mainstream Australia. The great dilemma facing modern Australia is the one million Australians who want more hours of work, particularly the "34% of underemployed part-time workers aged 15-19 who have experienced insufficient work for one year or more" *(Participation in Job Search and mobility,* Australian Bureau of Statistics, February 2017).

Unemployment, underemployment and youth employment must be the foundation of Catholic social justice concerns, yet the Church is largely invisible in this space. How does a Church speak honestly on the value of marriage, raising a family, home ownership and participation in Catholic life when it is muted on the foundational question of work? The Australian community is largely sympathetic to the past accomplishments of thousands of Catholics and their direct focus on the needs of mainstream Australia. Hospitals, education, nursing homes, palliative care all attest to this energy and purpose. Now is the time for a serious reconnection with the mainstream. Where better to commence than with our talented young Australians who desperately need support in entering the workforce and making a contribution to our nation.

Welfare lifestyle emasculates Australian Sudanese men

There is a great deal of discussion in Victoria at the moment over the emergence of young African crime gangs notably those such as the APEX gang, who have engaged in vigorous car-jackings, home invasion and have a swillingness to use significant violence in encounters with unarmed Melbournians.

The youthfulness of these gang members has caught Victorian Police and magistrates by surprise, often resulting in ineffective police and court responses. In November 2013 a magistrate expressed shock at the behaviour of a group of 17 year old Sudanese youths armed with guns, hammers and crowbars who conducted a string of robberies on service stations and 7-Eleven stores. These young men were nevertheless bailed and returned into the Victorian community.

Whilst it is customary to be critical of the Victorian police and justice system, for an obvious ill preparedness, they are not responsible for the rise and development of such gangs, particularly in the Sudanese community. That responsibility lies elsewhere.

For seven years (2005-2012), I was privileged to work within a parish community with over 100 Sudanese Australians. From the outset this community has struggled to adapt to Australian ways, yet solutions that I advocated were universally derided and ignored by welfare providers and local councils.

In a patriarchal Sudanese community we ignore a basic reality: give a Sudanese father the dignity of work and you demonstrate to his children his success in Australia and thereby encourage them to follow his path. In practice we took away his dignity, and ensured that when he tried to correct his teenage sons he would be mocked as an unsuccessful loser. The young Sudanese men now involved in gang-crime throughout Melbourne have not rejected Australia per se, but the pathetic path of fathers left with no work, no dignity and no influence! Who wants to follow that!

Many Australians, including many Catholics, continue to advocate for a welfare system that is unsuccessful in its essence and construction as it fails to keep families together, it destroys male confidence and erodes any relationship with his children. Nothing is more destructive in the Australian welfare system than the subconscious message that women and children can survive without fathers. Boys in these circumstances don't find manhood from the example of a father but in the transferred macho circles of the pub and gangs. Then, unsurprisingly, they irresponsibly father another generation of children with whom they will have little or no connection. Over the years these men will live with a series of women without marrying any of them or committing to their children in any serious way.

The great welfare challenge for Australia at the moment is the serious matter of getting males into work, work that will allow them the dignity of forming a family and modelling their children on success. The migrant story of the past is one of magnificent success, yet without those former paths of entry-levels work for fathers, we have little chance of replicating such success in the future. Sudanese Australians are not the problem, it's the continual welfare message that men don't count which ensures our current and ongoing difficulties. Whilst it is essential that women be encouraged to improve their lives and education in Australia, it cannot be at the expense of men.

What should the Catholic Church be doing?

Naturally, all of this begs the question: what should Australia's churches actually be advocating as social benefits for our community?

Pope John Paul II has given a powerful focus to the central issue confronting Australian society in the 21st century in his encyclical *Laborem Exercens*, highlighting the dignity and value of human work.

In a time of rapid economic and industrial change, Australia has not been immune from economic stagnation, the restructuring of manufacturing and the constant need to compete and adapt to global markets.

Catholicism must understand these processes and the needs of employment much better. Many churches have spoken endlessly about rights, particularly those for David Hicks, refugees and most recently the environment, but hardly ever about a fundamental religious understanding: vocation. What is it that you are meant to do in life? What is your unique contribution to others? How can you be true to yourself by serving others? This is a central aspect of faith, finding what God asks of you; finding your meaning in life and most importantly, acting upon it.

The difficulty with constant calls from Catholic leaders for respect and tolerance is that this does not provide an underlying sense of meaning and vocation. If we weaken the one group that provide this most profoundly, the Catholic Church, then we can hardly expect much beyond a society increasingly without boundaries, lacking self-restraint and desiring to serve our personal interests above all. At the heart of our mental illness and depression epidemic, marriage and family erosion and youth suicide tragedy rests a failure of the individual to find meaning and understand the true nature of freedom.

Over the last 30 years, Catholic churches have regularly raised with Government and their parishioners the need to be generous with our money. After all, the argument goes; we are a wealthy country with a responsibility to be good neighbours to countries in our region and locally with those less fortunate than ourselves. Sometimes, this is such a strongly applied principle that the very nature of the faith itself, can be rarely moved beyond "be generous to others as God has been generous to you".

Recently, there has however, been an increasing number of Australians who have come to question this entire premise. There is little evidence that giving local people welfare raises living standards in any significant measure, or that foreign aid does much to develop poorer nations over the longer period.

A snapshot of our region actually highlights another more vital reality; it is giving people work, developing local business, encouraging local entrepreneurs and giving the poor the means to create their own wealth that raises people out of poverty.

Australia has recently concluded a Free-Trade Agreement with South Korea (KAFTA April 2014) a significant player on the world economic scene but one that only sixty years ago was largely devastated by the Korean War (1950-53). It is not aid that has resulted in the South Korean transformation, it is a philosophy of economic freedom, a striving for excellence and an entrepreneurial class that has pursued wealth generating enterprise. Australians have also benefitted hugely from South Korean growth, our trade is worth around $30b (DFAT) and our citizens benefit significantly from their cars, TV's, electronic and other electrical goods.

Yet, South Korea, is only half the Korean story, North Korea is stringently opposed to economic freedom and ruthless in suppressing religious and political freedoms. North Korean restrictions breed massive starvation and poverty, yet South Korea free enterprise has raised fifty million from poverty to prosperity. Korea is but a tiny microcosm of the world, yet its basic principles hold true: Where people are given economic freedom, poor countries are more than capable of producing wealth. Without this freedom, North Korea awaits.

It is at this point that Australia's Catholics have a vital role to play. Currently, most discussions about poverty focus on the need for government intervention, the desirability of minimum wages and the necessity of increased welfare provisions. Yet, key components are missing from Church statements on poverty and welfare questions: How can Australia Catholics encourage the entrepreneur? "How do we support the essential role of business in providing employment? And how can we develop and support those who wish to start their own business initiatives?" In short, Australia's churches have underplayed the pivotal and indispensable component in moving people out of poverty: business support which leads to the provision of employment.

Part of the reason for such neglect appears to be a general mistrust of wealth creation in the capitalist system and a feeling that inequality and greed result.

A focus on the exceptional wealth of a few individuals often attributes to them selfish motives or corrupt practices. A more truthful analysis suggests that Australia's Catholic Church is also perceived as excessively wealthy, with secretive and self-protecting practices. It is not just millionaires within the capitalist system who may be tempted by greed. Communists, politicians, trade unionists, footballers, sheiks and bishops can also show themselves to be fragile human beings! Capitalist nations will always need the rule of law to ensure corruption is contained, but Samsung, Daewoo, Kia, Hyundai, LG and a host of others did not get to the point where they can employ thousands of people in both South Korea and Australia by corrupt and untrustworthy practices. They are successful by providing quality goods at affordable prices that modern Australians are keen to use.

For Catholics, humanity is made in the image of God with a fundamental call to be co-creators in the human future. Importantly it is God's direction to be "fruitful and multiply" that drives us not only to a creativity beyond the confines of reproduction, but to a full humanity with a vocation to safeguard our environment and to care and provide for each other.

Economics and work are not morally free environments. The

goods, services and employment they provide are essential to dignity, hope and a strong sense of self. In the fullness of faith and human flourishing work and enterprise are important components in the Catholic life. We quickly need to rediscover this truth.

How Catholics can really help the World's poor

The world's poor should always be at the forefront of the minds of all Australians, particularly its Christians who are driven by a moral imperative coming directly from the words of Jesus "whatever you do for the least of my brothers, you do for me".

It is time for Australian Catholics to take a hard moral and theological look at its responses to world poverty, focus on the truth of the world's situation and support viable and practical outcomes, not wish lists with zero realistic possibilities.

According to the World Health Organisation, over 3 billion people around the world still cook and heat their homes by burning wood and dung and over 1.2 billion people have no access to electricity. The uncomfortable truth is that demands for electricity in the developing world will increase dramatically as the movement of rural residents to cities continue apace. The United Nations has estimated that urban populations will increase from 3.9 billion people in 2014 to 6.4 billion by 2050. India is expected to acquire an extra 404 million, China 292 million and the African continents over 800 million by 2050. For India, that means an extra 1,281 people moving to cities per hour!

So here is another hard truth: the cheapest and most reliable form of electricity comes from coal generation! No if or buts, it is coal that has played a key role in reducing both the number of people in poverty but also other quality of life indicators, such as life expectancy, infant mortality, literacy and employment opportunities.

The International Energy Agency notes that world demands for electricity doubled in the last 25 years and the global consumption in coal from 2000-2014 increased by 65%. This was significantly greater than all forms of renewal energy.

Around 830 million people throughout the world gained electricity for the first time between 1990 and 2010, almost exclusively due to coal-fired generation.

There is no escaping the impact this has had on the world's poor. The safe storage of food and medicine, clean drinking water, the ability to heat and cool homes, improved transportation and development of business and employment opportunities.

Brett Hogan from the Institute of Public Affairs has noted in his Occasional Paper (June 2015) that two hundred years after the Industrial Revolution, coal is still responsible for over 40% of global power generation with new coal-fired capacity added every year. "The Australian Government's decision to increase coal supplies to India will permanently improve the lives of millions of people".

Nevertheless, opposition to coal-fired electricity still comes from many Catholics with some actually supporting radical climate change activism under programs pressuring companies to drop so-called "immoral investments". The Australian Greens have called for an end to all Australians coal exports by 2020, a ban on new coal mines and a further ban on all fossil fuel exploration. The immorality of such a position for the world's poor cannot be understated.

Catholicism has a strong focus on challenging individuals to support the common good. The practical reality of faith in Jesus should always be driven by humility, generosity and a wider community focus beyond ourselves. Nevertheless, Australia must be careful of attachment to those who suggest that developing nations cannot also enjoy the standards of living most westerners' experience, particularly those that advocate human population control. Both China and India have in the past advocated such solutions. Thankfully, both nations have now abandoned such nihilistic thinking.

In the next few years Australia and India will develop increasing economic and cultural ties. The number of Indian students currently studying in Australia attests to this. The basis of such a relationship must be focused on a number of agreed principles. India has the right to enjoy an electricity system that is reliable and cost-efficient. To deny other countries the living standard we enjoy is a moral and theological dishonesty.

Whilst Catholics also talk a great deal about poverty reduction, they are usually silent and blind to the obvious: gaining employment and holding it for a significant number of years is the key platform for human fulfilment.

Employment is the foundation of the whole social justice agenda, it is the means to provide for marriage and family, the ownership of a home and the resources to raise and educate children. It also allows for all of us to contribute to the welfare of our nation beyond our family and friends.

Central to any messages to our community must be that the demands of the modern economy do not destroy employment or the dignity of the worker. As John Paul II noted, Jesus spent most of his life working, hence, his call for "worker support whenever employment is threatened or lost, care for their families and a strong emphasis on new employment as central to our community life" (*Laborem Exercens*, No. 8).

Naturally, the world of work will always be in the midst of change,. The one constant reality of work is that nothing stays the same and adaptation is the key. All businesses must be focused on continued improvement and all workers on the need for adapting and developing skills.

Within the Australian political environment employment issues are directly related to the health of all Australian States. It is not just South Australia in which this is keenly felt. States that are unable to support their population with long-term employment which encourages individuals to build lives over a sustained period, will simply lose population to states which can.

Coupled with the provision of employment, the Catholic church also needs more understanding of the benefits that flow from free-enterprise. The generally socialist outlook that pervades church pronouncements is often restricted to the perverse idea that business is motivated by profit alone. Broader notions of wealth which include, physical, mental, moral and spiritual benefits almost always stem from the world of work.

Australian business, which employs most of us, has overwhelmingly allowed Australians to participate in the benefits and goods that define our humanity and has made an irreplaceable contribution to our society.

Last year the Business Council of Australia made a powerful call to lower company tax and personal income tax. Currently, Australia is at severe competitive disadvantage against our Asian neighbours, whose average corporate tax rate is around 22% compared to our 30% rate. Australian Catholics need a desperate re-think on the nature of poverty both home and abroad.

IV

A THEOLOGY THAT ERODES

Australian Christians across the political spectrum seem to have become strongly attached to the *ad hoc*, shoot from the hip style of leadership offered by the papacy of Pope Francis. The newly appointed Bishop of Parramatta, Vincent Long Van Nguyen is undoubtedly a fan, describing Francis as a breath of fresh air and in home spun Aussie style comparing his election to the shock of Michelle Payne winning the Melbourne Cup: "No one saw it coming no-one predicted it".

For The Bishop of Parramatta, Pope Francis appears as the fulfilment of all that Vatican II promised, "the launch of the Church into a new era of hope, engagement and solidarity" with the arrival of Pope Francis unambiguously signalling the commencement of this new era.

We can hardly criticise the Bishop too much for his immature enthusiasm for Pope Francis. Like most Australian church leaders, Bishop Long is struggling to find an authentic view with which to speak to the wider Australian society, yet he rightly recognises that we are at a critical juncture, "not only are we affected by such things as decline in Sunday worship, the fall in religious practice, the death of the priesthood and religious life, we also face the biggest challenge to date which is the loss of our moral credibility and trust capital due to the sexual abuse crisis" (*The Journal,* National Council of Priests, Summer 2016).

Sadly the interpretation that the Bishop offers is not one that is unique, radical or within the Christian tradition, but rather a view that is distinctly and sharply secular owing much of its genesis to the socialist and Green political movements. Bishop Long also suggests that the Church has entered into "a new exile and an inhospitable landscape where we must learn to walk with others, other faiths, other traditions, other voices including those who oppose us and are critical of us" (*The Journal,* National Council of Priests, Summer 2016).

To this "walking with others" the bishop begins with a veiled swipe at the Australian community itself, "Australia is a wonderful country, but where it is in terms of its treatment of asylum seekers, indigenous and marginalised people should trouble us" (*The Journal,* National Council of Priests, Summer 2016).

For Bishop Long, the significant history of the Australian Catholic Church, with its substantial work in hospitals, schools and nursing homes is held as belonging to little more than a "self-reverential church steeped in a culture of splendour. A church in stark contrast with the church of the poor and for the poor". What church the Bishop imagines Australia's only saint Mary Mackillop to have been serving when she provided significant Catholic education in isolated rural environments of Australia is hard to fathom. Such a view of the Australian Church downplays and insults the thousands of Catholic clergy and laity who formed this country and who worked selflessly in its emerging cities and towns.

The Bishop's critique of the modern church also leaves the faithful Catholic and priest of today with little in the way of pride for the recent past or hope for the future. "We cannot talk about the integrity of creation, the universal and inclusive love of God, while at the same time colluding with the forces of oppression in the ill-treatment of racial minorities, women and homosexual persons. It won't wash with young people when we purport to treat gay people with love and compassion and yet define their sexuality as intrinsically disordered" (*The Journal of Catholic Priests,* Summer 2013).

I hope perhaps one day the Bishop might recognise that the Church in Australia does not persecute or discriminate against gay people, what it does do is highlight the teachings of Pope Francis and the magisterium that marriage is between a man and a woman for the general good of children, family and society.

Bishop Long is, I'm sure, regarded in his diocese as a fundamentally decent human being, yet the theological distortions that form his thought have done immeasurable damage to the wider Australian Church and are a central reason why the Church has stopped speaking to mainstream Australia and consequently continues losing its ability to uphold, defend or explain its fundamental teachings in the public square.

For many Australian bishops, a vision of the "Church as a faithful remnant, a Church of the few, going into the future, bruised and hurting, yet somehow forming a new Israel after exile" (Pope Francis, *Joy of the Gospel*) is all that can be hoped for. This dystopian vision sees the Church without a voice in the public sphere, of minimal doctrinal integrity and without strength of purpose to argue for its place in the world as every previous generation of church has done. Such an Australian church has nothing to say to the key issues currently facing our society. What is a human being without the benefit of work? What do we make of a society so politically correct that free speech has no place in its environs? How do we challenge and correct a society that currently spends so much on itself that it dam's future generations to a diminished life.

The one great characteristic of all Catholic saints is a refusal to be limited and restricted in their service to others no matter what social rank and background. Without a church that will do this our Western civilisation itself is at fundamental risk. Perhaps the role of Australia's first saint is a timely reminder to the modern church – we are not called to limit ourselves but to transform the world.

This defeatist remnant theology has been championed by an American writer Rod Dreher who contends that many Catholics have already given up on struggling for their faith. For those who continue to hold the teachings of Catholicism he warns "we are on the brink of entire areas of commercial and professional life being off-limits to believers whose consciences will not allow them to burn incense at the Gods of our age" (Rod Dreher, *The Benedict*

Option). Dreher may well be correct that more and more young Catholics will find professions such as law and medicine off-limits to them. This has certainly been the experience of Catholics under communism, but surely these Australian circumstances demand a more vigorous response from Catholic leaders such as Bishop Long. A continued pessimism from bishops and lack of hope and vigour not only undermines young Catholics, but is a serious misreading of early church history.

Australian Catholics need to again take seriously Christ's command in Matthew 28: "All authority in heaven and on earth has been given to me. Therefore go and make disciples of all nations, baptising them in the name of the Father and of the Son and of the Holy Spirit and teaching them to obey everything I have commanded to you. And surely, I am with you always, to the very end of the age".

At no stage did the early Christians see separation from the world as a viable solution, nor were they debilitated by internal depression. These men and women experienced a Roman empire ruled by despots such as Tiberius, Caligula, Nero and Domitian, a world theologically opposed to them, yet their concentration on the words of Jesus won the world over. Perhaps also, the Australian Church should take note of the words of St Josemaria Escriva: "your ordinary contact with God takes place where your fellow men, your yearnings, your work and your affections are. There you have your daily encounter with Christ. It is in the midst of the most material things of the earth that we must sanctify ourselves, serving God and all mankind".

Evangelisation is the essential response to the virus of secularism. Cultural aberrations like secularisation will come and go just as the alleged unstoppable march of Communism (1917-1989) has come and gone. Catholicism is called to be lived not in fear but in vigour. That is the challenge for Australian Catholics.

V

SCHOOL CONFUSION

There are approximately 1,700 Catholic schools that form the Catholic education system in Australia. More than 80% of these are primary schools, which in most cases are what Australians recognise as the relatively small neighbourhood school attached to the local parish.

These schools, customarily do not cater for elite students, but form the basis of early education for over 700,000 young Australians. Up until the last 25 years, these schools were thought to be competent schools, providing a solid educational start along with a respected and restrained religious experience added into the mix. Nevertheless, in the last 25 years these schools are now widely recognised to be failing in two significant aspects.

Firstly, they are no longer acknowledged as a persuasive vehicle for the transmission of the faith, and, secondly they have predominantly failed as nurturing and invigorating environments for the development of Catholic culture, music, stories, art or self-respect.

The centre for applied Research in the Apostolate, a United States based group, found that 63% of those who had received a Catholic education, ceased to claim Catholicism as their faith between the ages of 10 and 17, a further 23% said they had left the faith prior to 10 years of age. Distressingly, only 13% said they would be likely to return to the Church.

Australian statistics on such disheartening realities are notoriously difficult to ascertain. However, we can be confident that circumstances in Australia are not dramatically different, given reports from Catholic organisation themselves alluding to severe difficulties within many Australian Catholic schools.

In 2007, the Australian Catholic Bishops published a pastoral letter entitled "Catholic Schools at the Crossroads". It called for Catholic schools to be "truly Catholic in their identity and life, centres of new evangelisation and led and staffed by people who will contribute to these goals".

The pastoral letter noted that non-Catholic enrolments had doubled in the last twenty years rising from 9% to 20% and continue to rise. The pastoral letter also recognised some debilitating deficiencies through its calls to strengthen:

- Staff who committed to the Catholic identity of the school;
- A Religious education program that is sound, attractive and professionally taught;
- Catholic schools that commit students to regularly take part in mass and reconciliation;
- Prayer to be included at assemblies;

- Crucifix and pictures of Our Lady visibly displayed; and
- Schools that are connected to the local parish and regularly invite the involvement of the parish priest.

Undoubtedly, these concerns raise serious issues of Catholic culture and practice that is not developed or expressed in many schools. Nevertheless, even these concerns fail to reveal the heart of the problem: Why don't Catholic schools produce children that love the faith? Or at least who are not aggressively rejecting its tenets? Overwhelmingly, there is a huge curriculum and cultural cavity that has not been addressed by many Catholic schools, even when the failure of these schools is well known.

In my view the Catholicism promulgated in many schools is a diluted, feel good, treat everyone equally, superficial faith, with no power to engage, empower, or change lives. Yet, even this is not the greatest problem – the primary problem is the disconnection between Catholicism and its two great off shoots.

These are the use of reason to solve problems and the cultural context of Western civilisation. In abandoning Western civilisation the church has dissolved the cultural setting which allowed it to thrive.

It has long been acknowledged that the study of history and Western civilisation is of central social importance. More than two thousand years ago, the Roman politician and lawyer Cicero warned "Not to know what happened before you were born is to be forever a child". Twenty centuries later, British Prime Minister

Winston Churchill counselled, "Study history. In history lies all the secrets of statecraft". Australian Catholicism suffers the consequences of not knowing its history, where it has been born and the positive consequences it has made to Western civilisation and culture.

Catholicism's central purpose is not to promote Western civilisation, yet in what way can we really conceive of a rupture between the two: without Christianity and Western civilisation where is Benedict, Thomas More, Ignatius of Loyola, William Wilberforce, Fyodor Dostoyevsky, Augustine, Caravaggio, Bach, Dante, Shakespeare, Hagia Sophia, St Paul's London, or St Peter's Rome!

The answer to Tertullian's famous question: "What has Athens to do with Jerusalem, is everything". In the same way, a Western Catholicism without Western civilisation cannot work, as it forgets the context in which it was born and in which it continues to interact.

Catholicism and Western civilisation are indispensably joined in the culture of the West: this is what Catholicism has forgotten and this is the basis of its loss of direction and loss of the young.

As an urgent commitment, we must underpin Catholic schools with a renewed dedication to teaching and expanding courses in Western civilisation and "Catholic history". It is not to downplay the culture and dignity of indigenous studies, but can we really imagine that anything but confusion will result – when students who know nothing of their own history, study small snippets of another. Is it also any surprise that many Catholic Schools produce children who not only abandon the faith, but come to see the Church as an institution of shame, in which they have little pride. A study of Western civilisation and Catholic centrality within it, is the key storehouse of our human experience and culture. As the Irish statesman, Edmund Burke argued "People will not look forward to posterity who never look backwards to their ancestors". In other words it is impossible to understand our faith and culture if we have no knowledge or pride in what we have inherited from previous generations. It is absolutely no surprise that Australian children are bored, indifferent and abandoning Catholicism when we consider the complete abandonment of our history and culture in Catholic schools. It is no use the leadership of the Church being appalled over such circumstances. It is the schools themselves who have ensured this situation. Any Catholic school that devotes more of its curriculum to indigenous studies, than its own, is lost and will never produce faithful Catholics ... to what would we actually have them join? The truth of our cultural identity is that we are Westerners, not Asian, African or Aboriginal. The consequences of Catholic teaching is that we have fragmented our faith and culture. Young Australians have no knowledge of the foundation of Catholicism, the uniqueness of democracy, our shared culture with the United States, Continental Europe, the United Kingdom and the centrality of Christianity within each one. By all means study other cultures and ways of thinking, but not to ground young Australians in our own Catholic/Western history, is to ensure confusion and ultimately the demise of Catholicism in Australia.

The irresponsibility of many Catholic schools is readily on display for those prepared to look. In June 2017, year 4 students at St Justin's Catholic Primary (Western Sydney) were deceived by teachers into believing they would be removed from their families at the conclusion of school.

The resultant trauma and distress saw many pupils (aged 7 years) try to escape school at lunchtime. This blatant and foolish politicising of legitimate and necessary action in some refugee families is nothing more than left-wing activist educators depriving children of real knowledge to push their own political agendas. Unfortunately, the number of Catholic schools that now encourage primary age children to attend adult demonstrations in school time (using school buses) for causes that are often against Australian laws is increasing. Not surprisingly, primary aged children can be distressed by the acts of violence and abuse that sometimes attend such demonstrations.

In these "politicised" Catholic school settings, children are not taught that the settlement of Australia and many other countries was a good thing, they are not taught the values and institutions that have made Australia a stable and prosperous country for the millions that have immigrated here, and they are not taught the bright future that avails those who apply themselves to personal success, and community service.

In some Catholic schools, the politicisation of history now sees the beauty and overwhelming benefits of Australian life and Western civilisation only through the distorted lenses of race, gender and sexuality.

In 2016 students at Melbourne University demanded the renaming of the Richard Berry building. This world famous anatomist, neurologist and anthropologist, who revolutionised the teaching of anatomy in Victoria also had an interest in eugenics. For the perceived sin of racism, Melbourne University has now erased Berry and all of his achievements. This level of unintelligent behaviour is beginning to permeate Catholic primary schools. Catholic opinion does vary over many political issues, this is all fair and reasonable in democratic Australia. Nevertheless, the Catholic education system does have a duty to uphold Catholic values and understandings, faithfully teach them accurately to Australian students and promote a truthful and proud understanding of their remarkable benefit to both the individual and our society.

VI

LOSS OF THE PUBLIC SPACE

Australian Catholicism has become almost invisible from public discourse in modern Australia. An aggressive secularism now dominates most Australian institutions, the media and the majority of the nation's educators, politicians and under 30 year old Australians.

The dominant ideology now prevailing in modern Australia, seeks to exclude any public exposure to the Catholic Church or any kind of visible role in the public sphere. Australian secularism only tolerates the church if it remains hidden behind the walls of parish or family home. Any attempt by the church to project a voice into social affairs or political life is ruled out or begrudged.

Undeniably, this is a difficult environment in which the Church finds itself, but it is also a condition to which the Australian church has contributed immensely through repeated acts of self-harm.

The sexual abuse of children under the age of consent by priests has occurred in most Western nations. This harrowing breach of trust has received a great deal of negative publicity and justifiably significant hostility to local church authorities and the

Vatican. From 2001 to 2010, the Holy See considered sex abuse violations involving over 3000 priests and dating back over 50 years. This criminal behaviour indicated patterns of long-term abuse, along with the church leadership's regular pattern of covering up such abuse. The Australian Royal Commission into institutional responses to child sexual abuse found abuse claims against ten Catholic religious orders, with four of these, registering offences against more than 20% of their members. These are horrendous crimes and the Church deserves all of the condemnation it has received for its failure to halt and correctly rectify these grave offences.

Nevertheless, greater censure should be levelled at Australian Catholicism for the complete failure to read the sign of the times. Australian society has been forgoing Catholic practice and disregarding its values long before clergy abuse scandals became regular news. The failure to adjust to the new reality of Australian society is as much an oversight as the continued lack of awareness still prevalent in the Catholic leadership. There is a severe disconnection between the Church and its host society. The continuing blindness to this disconnection is at the heart of Catholic inability to address the loss of a voice in the public sphere.

In recognising that Australian Catholicism is disconnected and largely irrelevant to the lives of most Australians I am not advocating for an Anglican/Protestant adoption of progressive causes, in the hope of being granted a public voice. Emeritus Pope Benedict XVI has rightly noted that the world does not need another progressive

Christian sect fixated on transitory politically correct causes. What it needs is the courage to put forward Catholic beliefs and values that are clearly defined and presented in ways that distinguish the Church from the surrounding society. In many parts of Australian Catholicism an alignment with leftist politics and shaky economics has failed to distinguish Catholic views from irrelevant Protestant ones. The vocation and task of the Catholic Church is not about causes, but presenting the faith and supporting the aspects of Australian culture it has created and given to Western civilisation.

Young Australians, particularly those under thirty, are almost universal in their rejection of the Church. Unfortunately, Australian Catholicism reinforces its own marginal status with young Australians by doing nothing to understand the phenomenon, or seeking to correct it. Yet, there are clear indicators of what this is about and substantial ways to challenge it

Firstly, it has nothing to do with perceptions the Church is full of old men out of touch with under 30 year olds. The recent significant election support for Bernie Sanders in the USA (76 years old) and Jeremy Corbyn (68 years old) in the UK (from under 30's and first time voters) suggest the message and delivery is what's lacking. Both these men also displayed a "popular" touch, almost totally absent in the current Australian Church leadership.

Primarily, the problem facing young people is insecurity in the job market. Unsurprisingly, when jobs dry up socialism rebounds, particularly for new job entrants who look for security and for whom a ready explanation for their failure in the job market can be blamed on "unfairness" or "inequality". A Catholic Church which was active and at the coal face would quickly have an enormous impact on young Australians perceptions. If we don't "do" anything, or offer anything to young Australians, how do we propose to impact their daily lives? This is not the primary business of the Catholic Church, but it is a necessary first step.

An Australian Catholic Church which continues to focus on fashionable activism like refugees and climate change will continue to see its churches stand like museums.

Over the last fifteen years, democratic principles and a general regard for democracy has deteriorated amongst young Australians. A new perception has evolved, which views democracy as enshrining unfairness and increasing the wealth and security of a select few. On any economic or social measure in the last twenty years this is glaringly incorrect. We continue in Australia to be wealthier and healthier year by year, yet for younger Australians an insistence upon greater equality has taken root.

For younger Australians democracy is not seen as delivering outcomes of change, and when Archbishops deliver statements to vote in particular ways, without previous engagement or debate, the Church is seen as part of the problem. In substantial ways, younger Australians have turned away from democracy, seeking change, through demonstrations, boycotts, pressure on companies, campus disruption, social media, all designed to emphasise greater equality: economic equality, marriage equality, gender equality, racial equality, Palestinian equality – the type of equality is almost irrelevant, the perception of inequality is to be fought on all occasions.

The hard truth for Catholicism is that its teachings will have little ability to penetrate the obsession with equality and diversity, particularly, if it imagines it can deliver pronouncement from authoritarian positions. Where are the Archbishops/Bishops in school and youth forums delivering a Catholic view on various issues? Irrelevance can also be earned by laziness or fear. The Church as it found in the first century AD can only grow and develop from the marketplace and from a spirit of humility.

The Church is not a democracy and its central role is not to support democracy. In fact, the Church has often recognised that a democratic process which is slavishly obedient to the whims of the people usually delivers less freedom and ultimately persecution for the Church. The Church, however does have a strong interest in institutions and organisation which counter balance central power.

The importance of the Church reclaiming this counter-balancing function is witnessed in the 2017 Federal Government submission on "The Status of the Human Right to Freedom of Religion or belief". Freedom of religion should not be taken as a given. This right will be challenged in forthcoming years, especially if the opinions of former Tasmanian anti-discrimination Commission, Ms Robin Banks, are in any way representative of community values.

Ms Banks is the Commissioner who accepted a complaint against the Catholic Bishops for articulating their belief that marriage is between a man and a woman. Her submission to the "freedom of religion inquiry" states, "whereas in private people should be largely free to practice their religion and beliefs, in the public sphere it is important to ensure the infringement of other rights do not occur as a result of the manifesting of religious or other beliefs".

This standpoint, which advocates for freedom of religion only in the private sphere would appear to contradict article 18 of the United Nations International Covenant on Civil and Political rights which "prohibits religious discrimination except in the interest of public safety, order, health, or morals or the fundamental right and freedoms of others". Ms Banks, however seeks to advance her restrictions directly into the private practice of churches when she notes "I do not support exemptions being made available to religious bodies and organisations when they refuse to make a facility available or provide goods or services for the purpose of solemnisation of marriage between two persons other than a man or a woman". This position is a fundamental denial of a religious organisations right to conform to its own doctrines, tenets or beliefs. It would ensure those beliefs take secondary position to the rights of any individual or couple claiming discrimination. The Catholic Church in Australia must act quickly, making a strong public case for its rights to propagate the faith in the public domain and use its own facilities in ways it sees fit.

Noting a change in attitude of many young Australians, a political and legal environment with a strong focus on equality and questions of discrimination, Australian Catholics must swiftly wake up to this new environment, understanding those organisations that now advocate against it and undertake new ways to counteract such viewpoints.

In brief terms there are a number of apparent disconnections between the church in Australia and various institutions which demonstrate the loss of Catholic influence in Australian public life.

Media: The church is a very poor media performer. Whilst it does endure significant and hostile forums in mainstream media, it is lacking in a positive story worthy of promotion to wider Australia. It should give significant thought to establishing and operating its own media outlets.

Hostility of Government and local councils: State Governments have proven increasingly antagonistic to conservative forces including the Church. Victorian State legislation in 2008 amended the abortion laws to allow for abortion beyond 24 weeks upon the consultation of a doctor who reasonably believes that abortion is appropriate in the circumstances. The Safe Schools Program which seeks to create inclusive environments in schools for same sex, intersex and gender diverse students will be compulsory in Victorian schools from 2019. The program encourages cross dressing, teaches students gay and lesbian sexual techniques and integrates gender theory across all subjects. Many local councils no longer decorate their buildings or suburbs at Christmas for fear of giving offence. Darebin Council in Victoria, holds no official Christmas functions, but does for Islamic celebrations. The Catholic Church has been unable to prevent such developments through either lack of influence or indifference.

The Church is not involved in sports or clubs: The Church currently has no involvement in sporting associations, young people's clubs or kindergartens. The Catholic primary school sports association does operate events, but does not compete outside of school times. The CYMS (Catholic Young Men's Society) movement has collapsed. This situation reduces its contact to those outside the Catholic school system to virtually nothing.

The Church's reputation and character is regarded as unconvincing in mainstream Australia: Unfortunately, polls and public perceptions continue to rank clergy and the Church very low on public trust. A 2016 MORI UK poll found that hairdressers are thought less likely to lie than clergy and that teachers, doctors, scientists, judges and police were all considered more trustworthy than clergy. Australian polls (Roy Morgan 2017) found the lowest levels ever recorded for clergy. Naturally the huge media focus on historical sex crimes by clergy has not helped. Nevertheless, the Church still has issues in relation to public comment that is not followed by action. Perhaps the most foolish example is that of the Anglican Dean of Brisbane who with great public fanfare declared his Cathedral would be open to refugees as living quarters. Naturally, when his diocese does nothing financially, provides no accommodation or support work for refugees, the Dean's enthusiasm was widely condemned. This senseless clergy behaviour continues to fuel perceptions that churches are unprofessional, irrelevant and quick to judge on subjects about which they know nothing.

Indifference to the workplace, business concerns and unemployed Australians: The most serious example of Catholicism's loss of influence in the public space is the Church's indifference to working Australians. The disregard of this critical issue ensures tnhat Catholicism has no ongoing contact, care or concern with working Australians. The acquiring and maintaining of employment is the basis of all that Catholicism sees as foundational to human life: marriage, financial security, raising children, a Catholic education and support for community life. It is therefore, disquieting that Australian Catholicism has such impoverished contacts with Australian business, operates no programs that encourages entry into the workforce (particular for young Australians), has no training opportunities for job seekers and has insignificant union contacts. Unless Australian Catholicism can undertake to prioritise this crucial mainstream community concern it will continue to see itself disregarded as a national organisation of importance.

VII

OUR CURRENT IDEA OF WELFARE HARMS CATHOLICISM

As a Catholic priest who walks the streets of Melbourne, rides its trams and always wears clerical attire, I am identified by beggars and homeless people as an easy target from hundreds of metres away. This scenario never gets any easier, particularly if there are crowds of people around and my thoughts turn to "what will bystanders think of me as a priest if I fail to give to the poor", and I myself am running a commentary of "does this individual look like a drug or alcohol user". Of course, in these short encounters with street beggars, it is easy to forget the larger more challenging questions. How can I really help the poor? Are there any long term solutions? And how can we as a society approach the whole question of charity and welfare?

The Catholic Church has always been concerned with the central goal of supporting and encouraging every individual to flourish to the full capacity of their hopes and abilities. This is a key definition, helping people to their full capacity must mean a lot more than just providing sufficient material goods to help them survive. Historically, the Catholic Church has been the prime initiator of hospitals, schools, orphanages, universities, palliative care and drug and alcohol rehabilitation – none of this has been undertaken because individual survival was considered the highest possible outcome. For Catholics, the individual is endowed with a unique dignity, combining a set of exceptional talents, capacities and futures. This idea of humanity is deeply rooted in the great love that God has for all of his creation.

The disaster for modern Australia is that our current welfare state is a secularised and materialistic shadow of what Catholics have always seen as the central purpose of charity: the flourishing of human potential. The modern Australian welfare state inspires no-one, doesn't change lives and leaves its recipients as virtual non entities, living the same humdrum lives and requesting more and more of unchanged services year after year.

For most welfare recipients their experience is one of distant bureaucracy, fuelled by disinterest and inefficiency, of work programs and courses that never lead to work and of a quiet descent into disconnection. It is as Pope Benedict XVI has described "a mere bureaucracy incapable of guaranteeing the very thing which the suffering person – every person – needs, namely loving personal concern" (*Deus Caritas est*, 2015).

In the modern Australian welfare system "a socialist vision of wide-spread government redistribution replaces private charity, ensuring that the poor do not have to depend on benevolence. Paying taxes replaces individual involvement in charitable work and the State becomes the charitable resources of first resort, crowding out the traditional institutions that once cared for the vulnerable"

(Marvin Olasky, *The Tragedy of American Compassion*, 1992).

A serious consequence of this kind of welfare state is the practical removal of the father from the life of the family. Over the last 30 years of Australian welfare provision the State has replaced the father's role of provider and protector, giving men no incentive to remain involved with the family or real ability to contribute the family life. The continued erosion of male employment actually creates a perverse incentive for young single mothers to avoid marriage in an effort to retain higher benefits. The great losers in this disintegration of family life is naturally the children.

Within Australian society, single motherhood is now socially acceptable. I am not recommending a return to disapproval of such families. I am only suggesting we should not be surprised at the rise of non-resilient demotivated and disengaged youth. There are two great dilemmas for the Australian Catholic Church in the current welfare environment. The more we fail to support Australian families, especially at a local level, the less resilient they grow and the more they are thrust into the hands of government. The serious consequence for them and the Church is that Catholicism fails to provide the moral and spiritual encouragement they need. The Catholic Church through its parishes must be more engaged and targeted in its practical and spiritual support for families.

Additionally, our failure to engage with young Australian families sees the government take on a greater role within these families. This secular experience usually results in the destruction of the faith and sees the Church forced out of another dimension of

Australian life. The Catholic Church has a profound and specific understanding of the family. If we do not advocate for that unique understanding, we can hardly complain about loss of influence within Australian families.

In its current form the welfare work of Australian Catholics is extremely dissipated. It has a secular framework at its heart, that is, we are exclusively focused on the material needs of struggling Australians. We have forgotten the idea that we are not social workers, but bearers of the good news of Christ. This does not mean that we should behave like street evangelists, but it does mean that our unique charisms should be deeply included in all that we do. Of particular importance in Catholic theology is the ability to journey alongside local people. The model of distributing welfare from centralised outlets has never been a Catholic success story. The example of Saint Mary Mackillop and her sisters is a more authentic Catholic model.

These sisters were prepared to follow farmers, railway workers and miners into isolated areas, live as they lived and provide education to their children. Because we no longer use the parish system to search out local needs we are fundamentally disconnected from welfare recipients and what their real needs may be. We also have given up on the idea of bringing Christ's message to them.

As a former Anglican, I am well acquainted with the collapse of that church, which over the last 30 years has pursued a social agenda focused on the rights of women, refugees and indigenous Australians. These social causes do have significant value in their own right, but they have been pursued using feminist and racial critiques, constantly seeking to challenge the alleged patriarchy of the church. The result has seen distortion of welfare into a few narrow paths and an ignorance of the real issues facing Australians.

The effects of such advocacy has been to empty the pews and concurrently fail to attract new people. Young Australians have seen these "agendas" as irrelevant to their needs and desires for a greater spiritual and ethical framework.

In recent years the Catholic Church has shown a strong propensity to follow the failed narrative of the Anglican Church. Our complaints to government never gets beyond the neurotic focus on refugees, aboriginal issues or the latest obsession of climate change. The central problem facing Australians of economic security, employment and growing the economy is entirely overlooked.

Those Catholic priests who shamelessly promote liberal social causes from the pulpit and neglect any mention of Christ are regrettably ensuring that Catholicism within Australia stumbles along the path to oblivion already taken by Anglicans.

The alleviation of poverty is a complex difficulty. Nevertheless, it does require the character of the Church to return to its former role and function. That is, the Church must provide hope and confidence from being alongside local people. It requires the Church to highlight a work ethic, honesty and a sense of responsibility. These are the factors which strengthen an individual to hold a job, stabilise a family and contribute to society. When the

Catholic Church fails to do this, poverty is easier to fall into and harder to climb out of.

The Catholic principle of subsidiarity holds that needs are best met locally – what is more local than the parish? Subsidiarity also holds that higher order should not interfere with the lower. The recent practice of centralised Catholic agencies has not delivered a good outcome for welfare recipients, for parishes, nor for wider Australia.

In recent years when local parishes have become blind to the needs of those who live in their midst, their usual call is that government needs to do more. Ironically, the call of Christ was "they do not need to go away, you give them something to eat" (Matthew 14:11).

Alleviating poverty through local support and improving people's lives has some chance of success when local Catholics and those in need have personal connection and loving concern. Catholic Welfare has no chance of success when we create bureaucracies and concentrate only on "survival" services – in this sense we are no different from secular government agencies.

Building welfare provisions on the subsidiarity concept is respectful both of social relationships and of local knowledge. It is not just directed to individuals but strengthens local community connectedness. Government welfare, on the other hand undermines community and accelerates its breakup.

Australian Catholicism is in a crisis both in its understanding of welfare and in its relationship with Government over issues of welfare. On the whole Australian Catholicism has now debased and undermined its unique understanding of how to help others and evolved into just another provider of "institutionalised" welfare.

This state of affairs hinders the mission of the Church as servant to the World. In its place the church has become another lobby group operating in a secular political domain that neither understands nor respects concepts of mission. This is a catastrophe for the Church as it divorces local Australian Catholics from a rich source of spirituality, denying the drive and energy that enlivened individuals such as Mary Mackillop.

As the Church has become more imbedded into its role as a "secular welfare" provider, many of our religious orders and welfare agencies have lost their way. Their moral radar has become increasingly divorced from the actual needs of Australians to be focused on narrow causes without wider appeal. Increasingly Australians are relying more and more on the State to meet their welfare needs and organisations called "Vinnies" are indistinguishable from any other provider. The unique Catholic understanding of faithful individuals energised as personal, moral actors for the good of church and society needs to be resurrected.

VIII

A SUCCESSFUL EXAMPLE: POLAND

STRENGTH UNDER ADVERSITY: THE POLISH SUCCESS STORY

Throughout the German occupation of Poland during World War II, Polish Catholic clergy were subjected to aggressive methods of imprisonment and extermination. Later the Soviet regime sought to eradicate what it meant to be Polish altogether, and the Church received special attention. But even in this most repressive environment, the Church in Poland was a steadfast defender of Christian European values and individual liberty.

Contrast this with the Catholic church in Australia. In a far more hospitable environment, its leadership has become less concerned with Christian pieties, and obsessed instead with leftist dogma. From centralised government, higher taxes and an undue focus on environmental issues, many Australian churches promote a Greens view of the world. Sadly, this means that our churches are talking less about individual freedoms and more about policies that would hurt the poor.

The courage of Poland's Catholic Church is remembered as an inspirational movement to save an entire nation from the horrors of Communism. Australian Catholics can learn a lot from this legacy.

Strength under adversity

Both German and Soviet invaders viewed Catholic clergy as a leadership group of National Resistance, fighting their planned extermination of Polish culture and faith.

Following the German-Soviet Non-Aggression Treaty, Poland was invaded by Nazi Germany on 1 September 1939 and by the Soviet Union sixteen days later. These campaigns ended with both countries dividing and annexing Poland. Both Germany and the Soviet Union sought the short-term goal of destroying the Polish State and the heinous long-term destruction of Polish consciousness as a unique and separate people.

Of the 10,017 Catholic priests serving in Poland in 1939, 2,647 were killed under German and Soviet authority.

Following the war, communists rule was imposed across all of Poland and tensions between church and state continued.

Whilst Polish communists were hostile to all autonomous organisations, the Catholic Church was its primary focus for abolition given that atheism is an inherent component of Marxist ideology. Polish communists clearly viewed Catholicism as a false and malevolent faith that acted as a barrier to the full acceptance by ordinary Poles to alleged communist betterment.

The communist government immediately enacted extreme restrictions on Catholic publications and actively closed Catholic organisations working in the wider society. Many priests, Catholic teachers and lecturers endured constant surveillance, arbitrary arrest and beatings and suffered personal attacks in State media.

In these organised assaults on Catholicism, the Polish Communist Party recognised that Catholicism acted as a powerful agent in forming and sustaining national culture. The Church as an institution carried out a central role as patron of cultural endeavours and acquired a reputation forged under German and Soviet rule for the defence of the Polish language and Western cultural traditions.

Under communist rule, revisionist historians tried to remove Catholicism from all literature and historical works. In falsifying Polish history and literature, communists hoped to cleanse the culture of religious achievements and ideas thereby making the process of secularisation easier.

Paradoxically, Catholic support for traditional values and culture found support amongst large numbers of non-believers. Catholic defence of civil liberties, whilst centred around religious freedom, also fought against all forms of coercion imposed by governments on individuals and social groups.

The clear Catholic defence of traditional values impacted

significantly on Marxist claims which usually centred on issues such as "equality" and alleged "exploitation". Importantly, Catholics were able to regularly point to the despotic tendencies of communist bureaucracy and the stultifying nature of communist life and cultural expression.

The Polish expression of communism lamentably prompted a serious number of deep social concerns. Alcoholism, abortions and divorce all proceeded to approach critical levels. In addition, the prospect of finding tradesmen, nurses, doctors or even police prepared to attend the needs of their wider community, without financial incentives, was a constant concern.

The battle of ideas

This situation encouraged Catholics to refocus their local parishes into centres with an increased emphasis on support, compassion and cooperation among people. Catholic lifestyle became a notable contrast to the chaos and disorder that affected many individuals demotivated in their daily contact with Polish communism.

Over time, Polish communism modified its stance towards Catholicism, recognising its right to exist in principle yet seeking to make that existence a purely private and individual matter. The place of Catholicism within the public sphere was still aggressively criticised and resisted. The Catholic conviction that religious practice ennobled human conduct in community life, business, culture and politics was not one ever to be accepted by communists. In response, Catholics initiated a whole range of programs, such as retreats, public talks on Catholic topics, summer camps and friendship groups for university students. All of these activities sought to stimulate and encourage intellectual discourse over the challenges facing Poland.

It should also be noted that Catholic priests were encouraged by their bishops to engage in these kinds of intellectual endeavours. Liturgical and pastoral responsibilities remained as primary concerns, yet priests were also expected to work with small communities on intellectual and creative responses to problems confronting Polish society. The "weeks of Christian Culture" initiative saw the Church incorporate music, theatre, films, dance, poetry talks and Mass into a format that both celebrated Polish culture and Catholicism's place within it.

Polish resistance to national socialism and communism was led by a Catholic Church that was unashamedly rooted in Western ideology. It advocated for free speech and a separation of powers that highlighted the church's rightful place in society, yet a place unhindered by government control. The Church importantly saw these fundamentals as bound strongly to the outcomes they produced: civic engagement, private rights and the equality of women.

A stark contrast

The accomplishments of Polish Catholicism could not be in starker contrast to what we are currently witnessing in the fragile churches of Western Europe and Australia.

The European Union is continuing to spend way beyond its means. An increasing number of bureaucrats, consultants and unelected officials, pass thousands of new laws that enshrine permanent deficits. And where are the churches? Almost totally silent and distracted with environmental causes over which they have no influence and which have demonstrably proven to have hurt the poor.

Throughout Europe, home heating costs have tripled, real wages are depressed and poorer Europeans spend more than 10% of their income on energy. The high cost of renewable energy sees around 300,000 German households cut off from electricity each year due to unaffordable costs.

In nations where taxation, spending and borrowing rise each year, climate change is not seen by struggling Europeans as the main game. Employment, border security and cultural integrity are the factors that centrally impinge on daily life.

In a Europe where illegal immigrants can regularly and successfully appeal against deportation on flimsy grounds such as human rights violations (examples include lower health care in home countries being claimed as potential torture and successful grounds for resisting deportation) there is now a strong disconnection between European government and its citizens. Unfortunately, the position of European churches in also championing a rights, refugee and environmental agenda has also ensured a disconnection between church and parishioner.

Australian churches show a profound tendency to mimic their

European cousins, yet the current state and influence of Australian churches are perhaps at their lowest ebb in our nation's history. The statistical evidence points to a decline for some churches where recovery is becoming impossible. Anglicans admit that six of their diocese from a total of 23 are currently unviable and all but one or two are in deep financial chaos. Reviews over why this "new reality" has occurred are unable to move beyond superficial laments over the rise of secularism and commercialism.

Yet, the acute disconnection between Australian churches and ordinary Australians is at the heart of this loss of influence and demands a deeper and more honest appraisal.

Emblematic of this disconnect has been the decision in recent years for various Australian churches to "divest" from fossil fuel companies. It's not objectionable on its face for a Church to refuse to invest in firms that go against their faith, but the decision from the Sydney Anglican Church to withdraw its then-$262 million investment fund from resource stocks in June 2015 was a pointless symbolic gesture. The trustees of the Church fund – and of the other church funds which have made the same decision – should be making investment decisions to maximise returns to reinvest in the Church to fund its core activities in their communities.

The decision of St John's Anglican Cathedral in Brisbane to offer "sanctuary to refugees" affected by a high court ruling that their detention on Nauru was lawful is a case in point. This was nothing more than a frivolous chase for a headline. Where are the refugee centres established by this church? Where is the purchased property that would allow refugees to live in proper facilities befitting their dignity? Where are the "refugee workers" established by these churches to nurture and care for refugee individuals and families? The diocese of Brisbane has none of these programs or initiatives in operation. When a church has no skin in the game, yet is determined to vigorously critique others, it loudly trumpets its disconnection from reality.

The need for church engagement

Australian society faces a number of core problems. Each of our major cities now has neighbourhoods where individuals and families have no jobs and little hope of improving themselves. These suburbs are marked by high rates of unmarried mothers, absent fathers, drug dependence and total reliance on welfare. Nevertheless, many Australian churches continue to call for increases in welfare provision while failing to recognise the central failings of the system. It is government regulation such as minimum wages which makes it so difficult for low skilled individuals to find work. How is it reasonable for churches to continue calls for increased welfare and yet totally omit to call for the abolition of impediments that are barriers to entry-level work?

Even the Australian branch of the St Vincent de Paul Society, an organisation ostensibly dedicated to serving the poor, argued before the federal election that the incoming government should commit to a "fairer tax system". In particular, the Society's CEO, Dr John Falzon cited negative gearing as a "cost" to taxpayers, and tax cuts for companies as a giveaway to the big end of town.

Unfortunately, this dismissive attitude to company tax is all too common in some Christian leaders. A lower tax liability for businesses means extra capacity to expand their activities, and to employ more people. For the head of St Vincent de Paul to ignore the positive economic effect of a tax cuts is a terrible dereliction of his duty.

A youth unemployment rate of 13% is a blight on all of us, yet again Australian churches have no commitment to this issue. Surely the promotion of employment is the foundation of the whole social justice agenda. Employment is the rock that provides for marriage and family, the ownership of a home and the resources to educate and raise children. Australian churches that continue to attack free markets and call for restrictions on job creation fail to understand that broader notions of wealth include the physical, physiological and spiritual benefits that stem from the world of work.

The Polish Catholic response to communism has much to teach modern Australian Christianity. This response advocates close contact with ordinary people, their problems and aspirations. Importantly, it also connects the faith with issues of freedom across a wide social spectrum, not just religious freedoms. It seeks courageously to defend people against injustice, violation of human rights, free speech, economic exploitation and other government abuses of power.

Perhaps centrally it suggests that issues of culture, Western civilisation and free speech are issues the Australian Church must again champion as it seeks to renew its divine mandate for all Australians.

IX

RECLAIMING A VOICE: RETURNING TO THE PUBLIC SQUARE

The Catholic Church claims to embrace the truth, applicable for all humanity, at all times and in all places. However this claim looks dubious if you look at the Australian Catholic Church in the twenty-first century. Catholicism has lost its confidence, abandoned important sections of Australia life and has no obvious plans for recovery. We need to move from a position of safeguarding existing structures to one where we vigorously promote and highlight our unique understanding of Gods intentions for the World and how we intend to fulfil them. Australian society, which is wrapped in self-indulgence, institutional and political breakdown and youth dissatisfaction needs us to do this. The Catholic voice is vital to Australia's long-term health and prosperity. Undoubtedly, the Australian Catholic Church is the only institution that can offer an attractive counter-culture truth to the cultural and societal confusion in which Australia finds itself.

Nevertheless, it is important that Australian Catholics begin to accurately understand the situation and to read the signs of the times. Large sections of Australian political and cultural life argue that the church should remain silent in the public sphere and some even wish for Catholic extinction.

In recent years, the overriding narrative surrounding the Catholic Church is one of clergy abuse. The Church has been unable to find or hold a sufficiently powerful and positive story to counteract the "abuse" narrative. Unless this can be achieved in the near future, we will continue to witness further loss of community trust and support and subsequently greater decline.

There are three essential aspects to reclaiming a Catholic "voice" within Australian society. The forming of a "new narrative" must have a doing or action dimension that stems from a robust Catholic sacred and religious life and our actions, purposes and devotions are firmly founded on Catholic culture.

If we are to significantly impact Australian society, these three dimensions must be unified. We must clearly be able to point to the "practical" aspect, highlight the "spirit" behind the action and then acclaim the "cultural" dimension as outcomes to draw Australians to the faith and energize our own communities.

An illustration of this "new narrative" might be the formation and development of work preparation programs for young Australians. This must not be outsourced to others and only funded by Catholic money, rather it must have "Catholic business" and "Catholic people" involved in its delivery who are willing to claim such an identity. These programs must be operated on Catholic premises or parishes with clearly marked structures which point to local Catholics.

Now is not the time to run programs in "hands off ways". We need firmly to identify, activate and vitalise our own people in this work. The model might be broadly implemented from diocesan frameworks, but the principle of subsidiarity must be claimed and adopted as local initiative. Further, the charism of the people involved must be proudly proclaimed and the Catholic culture dimensions of the program loudly highlighted. It should be obvious to all that this program is "Catholic local and highlights a unique Catholic gift or charism". To prepare young Australians for work is also a spiritual endeavour – addiction, alcoholism, family breakdown and depression demand that we highlight such connections. Without these connections we will fail to be "particularly" and "obviously" Catholic and suffer the loss of energy to sustain them. Too much of what we currently undertake is bureaucratic and impersonal, does not highlight subsidiarity and leaves our faithful communities with little to do. Catholics are known by what they do. If we could be known as effective providers of work programs for young Australians, we can be seen as continuing a traditional Catholic field.

We could claim a practical and theological support for the young and families and we could return to so many of our parishes new ways to proudly proclaim a faith that works, is local and supports society. The days of funding diocesan only initiatives should be ended. The propagation of Catholic culture must be an outcome in all that we do – Why? Because Catholic culture is the antidote to counter the rampant secularism of modern Australia. We must be clearly recognisable as distinct from government and secular agencies. Yet on many occasions this is not the case. Cloning the programs of others leads nowhere.

Pope John Paul II and the Polish Catholic church between 1940-1980 have led the Church in demonstrating not only the value and beauty of Catholic culture, but its direct and paralysing challenge to communism. Australian catholics who wish to challenge contemporary secular norms must do likewise. In unrivalled ways, Polish Catholicism asserted itself as stand alone culture, radically different from the stifling apathy and dullness of communism.

The Polish Church initiated their own theatres and put on plays featuring Catholic stories, bible themes and Catholic resistance throughout history. It employed playwrights, musicians and actors to specifically work on a continuous stream of ideas and it toured these theatre groups across the country. It also produced works which underlined the chaotic and costly human dimension of communism. It encouraged clergy and parishes to offer and spotlight better ways of living as community and it seconded any individual or group who was supportive of its broad themes. These theatres called attention to the centrality of family, the way faith impacts on ordinary life, the dignity of work, and the value of living moral lives.

There is no reason that internet and television cannot be used in similar ways, but overwhelmingly these initiatives should be local within communities and supported by local parishes. This Catholic action demonstrated, to both Catholics and non-Catholics alike, the depth of the faith, the importance of subsidiarity and the true centre of individual and community health. In the face of rampant abortion, erosion of family and individual breakdown through drugs, alcohol and loss of purpose, it was able to resurrect Polish society in the space of forty years.

Furthermore, Polish Catholicism also developed a free weekly newspaper to spread these stories, cultural initiatives and topical articles. This newspaper was central to counteracting the influence of the communist press, but it also focused on the everyday concerns of Poles; beauty tips, cooking, staying fit and medical advice could also be found in its pages. In noting how different Catholic culture was to communism, it also concerned itself with the needs and hopes of ordinary people.

In contemporary Australia, many sections of the Church are losing courage and melting away. A great deal of support is already needed in our schools, for our doctors, lawyers, business people, young people at university and our parishes. Some of these are close to collapse and need immediate help.

As a matter of urgency, the Church must consider the formation of revitalisation teams, small teams of priests and laity specifically designed to support and engage with struggling Catholic stakeholders. These small teams might spend 2-3 weeks in a different parish or school, specifically teaching and engaging with Catholics and other interested people over the issues that confront us. Overwhelmingly, the most important aspect of these "revitalisation" teams is that individual Catholics can find support and encouragement.

Many Catholics are struggling alone without a feeling that the Church is there to support them, and that their Church does not speak out on critical issues. Specific teams formed to engage with Catholic schools, parishes, to bolster Christmas and Easter in specific regions, to establish youth groups, or to work with clusters of Catholic families, stating very clearly that Catholic life is different, workable, offers support and resides within a distinctive cultural life, radically different from contemporary secular life. Of crucial importance is correcting our lack of connection to the world of work. This holds back the possibility to engage and understand the issues facing Catholics in the workplace. It also prohibits us from engaging creatively with non-Catholics. Work chaplaincies, business support and training programs are all examples of Catholicism bringing something to the table. In an increasingly, hostile world, which would deny and restrict Catholicism to a small number of fields, we need to be working to support our people.

In the new world of contemporary Australia, Catholicism must expect resistance and prepare our people for it. We must affirm our Church as a viable alternative to the current destructiveness of modern Australia and we must be more bold and more forceful in the public space. The Polish Catholic Church was never afraid to hold outdoor mass in public spaces, to fight for religious freedom and to contest vigorously in the world of ideas. The Australian Catholic Church of the future must do likewise.

X

AFFIRM AND PROMOTE FREEDOM OF SPEECH

The *Charlie Hebdo* magazine began publishing in 1970 with the stated goal of satirising religion and politics. Its attacks on Catholics were regular and on most occasions deeply offensive to the Church throughout France and wider Europe.

In 2006, the magazine reprinted a series of uncomplimentary cartoon depictions of the prophet Mohammad, resulting in substantial protests in many Muslim countries.

In January of 2015 a series of terror attacks took place in Paris against the magazine headquarters, alongside a kosher grocery store and the Paris suburb of Montrouge. A total of 17 innocent people were killed.

In the wake of these attacks Pope Francis spoke about the attacks, yet in ways that scandalised many world leaders and disappointed faithful Catholics. Pope Francis expressed a forthright view that there are limits to freedom of expression and that anyone who swears at his mother deserves a punch. Whilst the Pope noted that freedom of speech and expression are fundamental human rights, he also added his belief that there should be limits to offending and ridiculing the faith and beliefs of others. By way of example, the Pope stated "If my good friend Dr Gasparri says a curse word against my mother, he can expect a punch, its normal, you cannot provoke. You cannot insult the faith of others. You cannot make fun of the faith of others".

Serious difficulties arise from these statements of the Pope, particularly around free-speech that might be seen to be critical or offensive to others. Vatican silence on the harsh treatment of Christians in many Muslim countries is a case in point. When is it appropriate to speak out, or even defend your viewpoint if it risks a clash or giving offence to others? Vatican perspectives over the last five years suggest that their view is for non-criticism of other religions, even if persecution of others, including Catholics occur.

The issue of free-speech now appears to be a non-starter when discussing the behaviour of other faiths, yet the Vatican criticisms of particular politicians and political systems seems to be alive and well. The Vatican has recently criticised evangelical protestant Christians in the United States, along with Republican presidents including Ronald Reagan, George Bush Snr, George Bush Jnr and Donald Trump. The Popes personal support for the Marxist Venezuelan President Nicholas Maduro, who enforces a severe anti-democratic program, including arrest and detention of opponents has dismayed many Catholics. Nevertheless, Catholic doctrinal statements include powerful endorsements of freedom, the compendium of the social doctrine of the Church notes: "freedom is the highest sign in man of his being made in the divine image, it is a sign of the sublime dignity of every person. The right to exercise freedom, especially in moral and religious matters, is an inalienable requirement for the dignity of the human person". The Catechism of the Church, gives a little more flesh on the centrality of freedom. The more one does what is good, the freer one becomes. There is no true freedom except in the service of what is good and just. The choice to disobey and do evil is an abuse of freedom and leads to the slavery of sin".

In its teaching the Catholic Church has always sought to put freedom beyond the individual perspective, the uncontrolled exercise of one's own personal autonomy does not lead to freedom in its fullest self. Yet, surely, the Church must continue to speak freely against just such an attraction to the reduction of freedom. The abuse of drugs, alcohol, increases in crime and violence towards women are all examples of the erosion of freedom. In these instances the Church must have both the right to speak freely, but also the courage to do so.

Western society's current distortion of Shakespeare's mantra "to thine own self be true" has only ever been half of the solution, the right to speak out against injustice is the necessary Catholic counter-weight. When considering what Catholicism should be prepared to advocate within Western society, a number of basic human rights must be affirmed; The right to life., the right to live in a united family, the right to develop one's intelligence through education, the right to religious freedom and seeking the truth, the right to employment and to freely establish one's own family.

All of these rights are central to obtaining the fullness of humanity, yet they are all prefaced on another sometimes hidden right: the right to free speech. If Catholics are not free and strongly encouraged to debate, teach, argue, propose and sometimes criticise, then how can we sustain any kind of voice in the service of these great "benefits" of our faith. Without free speech, no democracy can function, but the same is true for the Catholic Church. Democracy is more than just a system that allows free elections, it has to be nourished and sustained by ordered public conversation. Attempting to ban or curtail free speech is a fundamental attack on the foundations of democratic life.

Whilst the Church does not understand itself in democratic terms, it also knows the experience of censorship and bans on free speech. Communist and socialist systems have always favoured censorship of the Church, that reality is alive and well in China, Vietnam and North Korea in our own day. Communists and socialists have always recognised the appeal of the Church as an oppositional force to totalitarian thinking. Hence, Catholic media, sermons, schools and conferences are always prohibited. The next step of exile, imprisonment and murder is never far behind.

Freedom of expression is undoubtedly under attack in Western societies, including Australia. The Church would be foolish to stand by and assume all will be well. We know from our history that the right to advocate for Catholic understandings and beliefs, indeed the Church's right to exist will be fundamentally challenged if free speech in nations such as Australia is eroded.

Christians who operate businesses in many Western nations are already under pressure to downplay their beliefs or face legal prosecution.

In the United Kingdom, husband and wife small business owners and practicing Catholics, Daniel and Amy McArthur were in 2015 ordered to pay damages to a customer for refusing to bake a cake with a pro-gay marriage slogan. Whilst this may appear a superficial issue, there are significant wider implications for all Catholics of legal rulings against freedom of conscience. Legal systems that require business people to promote ideas or causes to which they conscientiously object is detrimental to law, such law does not discriminatie against people, but against ideas. It is a fundamental task of the Catholic Church to promote its ideas and beliefs to all those prepared to listen. This is otherwise known as mission, unfortunately Australian Catholics has been silent on this issue for too long.

The condition of free-speech in Australian universities has also come under serious threat in recent years. The right to free intellectual inquiry is often now subjected to significant censorship, with those who hold allegedly "politically incorrect" views, not invited to speak or subjected to noisy demonstrations. Ironically it is often student representative bodies who engage in such tactics. Recently, the University of Technology, Sydney announced on Facebook that "same sex marriage should not even be a debate". Such views suggest that young Australians, who should readily be prepared to test and challenge ideas in public forums are no longer willing to engage with ideas they consider already determined.

The Institute of Public Affairs 2016 audit of free-speech on Australian universities found that 8 out of 10 implemented policies that weaken or erode free-speech. The reality for our universities is that people who disagree with a university or student body worldview will not be invited to speak or will be censored and bullied when they do. Melbourne University recently reached a new low, when it determined through a student union workshop, that unconscious bias was pervading university tutorials and seminars. The source of this bias was quickly found to be "white male" students. The university now advises male students that prior to speaking they should consider if their comments might "be self-aggrandisement or will they contribute to learning". The guidelines further suggests that "men should seek to speak more like women", in that they should not speak with "absolute confidence", but rather qualify their statements with phrases like "I'm sure that this is a good idea but...", additionally, male students should refrain from engaging in "Australian banter". All this puts Melbourne University a long way from the values of Martin Luther King who said that "people should not be judged on the colour of their skin, but on the content of their character".

Australian universities are also rigorously embarking on a program of "trigger warnings, a feature of American universities, in which students are warned that lectures contain material that might offend. Such warnings are now provided for subjects that might touch on racism, homophobia, disability, body image and certain foods. Warnings are also employed on the canon of Western literature where F. Scott Fitzgerald's *The Great Gatsby* is "misogynistic", Virginia Woolf's *Mrs Dalloway* speaks of "suicidal inclinations" and Ovid's *The Metamorphoses* describes "sexual assault".

Such warnings are at the level of extreme idiocy, nevertheless a deeper affect suggests that they condition students how to think on a particular work, prior to undertaking their own evaluation and reaching their own conclusions.

In most Western societies, left learning political parties and human rights groups view freedom of speech not as individual rights but as behaviour that needs government management and supervision.

The rapid growth of politically correct departments and officials within the public service, private companies and even sporting bodies are an outcrop of a desire to control and stifle some forms of speech and their underlying ideas.

The official Catholic standpoint is vastly different from these emerging practices in Australia. The Catholic tradition notes that human dignity is given from our shared image and likeness to God and that our equality is subsequently based on Canon Law and wider Western law. Our universities and our wider society need people with differing worldviews. This is the most effective way to deepen our understanding of problems, the thoughts of particular groups within society and the way we relate and engage with our regional neighbours and beyond.

However, the current position of the Australian church appears to be one of withdrawal and non-engagement. This posture places Catholics at a huge disadvantage in Australian community life. We cannot expect anyone to make the case for Australian Catholicism and our beliefs except ourselves. Catholics must know from our history that failure to engage with the world of ideas will only ensure increasing lies, disinformation and attacks on our faith and practices.

XI

AFFIRM WESTERN CIVILISATION

The average young Australian knows little of the practices, faith or teachings of the Catholic Church.

Many of this cohort will readily describe the church as a corrupted organisation, keen to protect its wealth, and unscrupulous in its protection of paedophile clergy often hiding them from scrutiny and prosecution.

The story of Catholicism for these young Australians is one of ignorance, repression and shame.

In consequence, it is an immense shortcoming of Australian Catholics that they are so reluctant to speak of their success or to note that the very foundations of our society are formed on Catholic understandings and practice.

Western civilisation is indebted to Catholicism for its education system especially universities, the sciences, legal principles, including the justice system and international law, along with charitable work including the development of hospitals and the hospice movement. The list of Catholic contributions to our society is endless, yet to our discredit these central concepts in the formation and sustaining of our society are utterly disregarded or ignored. Much of this failure rests with Australian Catholicism which appears no longer to support these magnificent achievements or hold sufficient pride in their embrace that would result in their teaching to our children.

The Australian Catholic Bishops have produced substantial statements on social justice on ecological issues, on doctrine and morals and on intra-religious affairs. Many of these statements are significantly critical of Australian community life. They have not as yet produced a document on the influential achievements of Western civilisation or the profound freedoms that stem from it.

Historically, the promotion of science, with its rigorous commitment to intellectual inquiry and scholarly debate was keenly supported by the Church. The work of Fr Nicholas Stern and Fr Athanasius Kircher have seen them designated as the Fathers of Geology and Egyptology respectively. Atomic theory is heavily indebted to the work of Frs Riccholi and Boscovich. There is no doubt that the Catholic Church contributed more intellectually and financially to the study of astronomy than any other organisation until the onset of the twentieth century. The role of the Catholic Church in science has been completely inverted to the point that many modern Australians believe the church to be anti-scientific inquiry and anti-rationality. This is a consequence of a church that has ignored and failed to promote its own history.

The establishment of Western law is largely an outcrop of canon law which was the first coherent and modern expression of law in Europe. Prior to this, the work of the Christian orthodox emperor Justinian I in reviving the corpus of Latin jurisprudence and including canon law dimensions had a profound influence on Western law.

The increasing emphasis on individual rights to be found in these developing forms of legal praxis are firmly based on Christian scriptural precedent, especially the thought of St Paul. "There is no longer Jew or Greek, neither slave nor free, nor is there male or female, for you are all one in Christ Jesus" (Galatians 3.28). The formulation of such "individual" rights comes exclusively from Western law and is not found in meaningful ways in other legal traditions.

With the decline of the religious contemplative life in modern Australia, it is now assured that the majority of Australians will never have encountered a monk or cloistered nun in contemporary life. The religious life of the Benedictines is still practiced notably at New Norcia in Western Australia, where the monks are still involved in farming.

This Benedictine farming tradition is the practice all over the world where the Rule of St Benedict reflects the connection between manual work and spirituality "Therefore the brothers should have specific periods of manual labour as well as prayerful reading. They must not become distressed if local conditions, or their poverty, should force them to do the harvesting themselves. Where they live by the labour of their hands, as our fathers and the apostles did, then they are really monks" (Rule of St Benedict, Chpt 48).

It is because of the work of these monks through a fifteen hundred year period that changing agricultural practices were able to thrive in many differing conditions. It is thanks to the knowledge of these monks that cattle breeding, agriculture and land clearing have developed in such beneficial ways.

Catholic charitable organisations and practices are perhaps the strongest dimension of the Australian Catholic Church in the eyes of most Australians. Catholic charity has no equal in the amount nor the range of its work. There can be no doubt that Catholic charitable work and concepts have totally shaped the unique Western view of suffering and a compassionate response to sickness and death. It is important to recognise that this Western tradition of mercy and service did not arise from good intensions but is based firmly on the scriptural commands of Christ "A new commandment I give to you, that you love one another as I have loved you. By this shall all men know that you are my disciples, if you love one another" (John 13.34-35).

Throughout history the practice of this dictum has caused a great deal of shock and surprise.

The French philosopher Voltaire, a notorious anti-Catholic, was still able to praise the charitable work of French Catholics. "Perhaps there is nothing greater on earth than the sacrifice of youth and beauty, often of high birth, made by the gentle sex in order to work in hospitals for the relief of human misery, the sight of which is so revolting to our delicacy".

During the fourth century the Roman Emperor Julian supported the restoration of Hellenistic polytheism as the State religion, and targeted legislation against wealthy Catholics with a view to driving Catholicism out of the public space. Nevertheless, even Julian could be shocked at the actions of ordinary Catholics "These impious Galileans not only feed their own poor, but ours also, welcoming them to their meals".

There can be no doubt that Catholic commitment to the poor and sick, sustained for over two millennium, represented a break with imperial and pagan thinking which previously emphasised a disinterested and emotionless spirit. Whilst this merciful and indiscriminate application to all in need is sometimes still criticised, there is no doubt that the charitable work of Catholics has been a profound source for good in Western society and beyond.

In the minds of many Australians the Middle Ages is held to be a desolate intellectual period, where knowledge was suppressed by a Catholic church in fear of losing its powerful grip over both monarchy and commoners. Nothing could be further from the truth, it is to the church of the Middle Ages that Western civilisation owes its greatest intellectual gift – the birth of the university system.

This system was radically new, it did not exist in ancient Greece or Rome and it is the Church that first encourages and financially supports the idea of extending the development and preservation of knowledge – as widely across society as possible. It is in this decision that another radical idea of meritocracy is born.

Again, it is in the scripture and the Rule of St Benedict that we find the source of such revolutionary ideas, "A freeborn man shall not be preferred to one coming from servitude, for whether we are bond or free we are all one in Christ..." (Rule of St Benedict, ch. 59).

In addition to fostering the "idea" of the university, the Church played a crucial role in their development of authority, rights and privileges and international connectedness.

At the onset of the protestant reformation, eighty one universities were in existence in Europe and thirty-three possessed exclusive Papal charters. The dominance of the church's university system is clearly seen in Pope Gregory IX, (1233) conferring masters degrees entitling the bearer to teach anywhere in the world. This privilege is the foundational idea of an international academic community.

The nurture and development of the university system rests almost exclusively with the Catholic church. Their prerogative is seen in the granting of charters, the recourse of universities in seeking church adjudication of disputes, the granting of world-wide teaching rights to academics and the fostering of largely unrestrained academic debate and discussion. No institution has contributed as much to educational life and the promotion of widely available knowledge and dissemination.

Whilst it must be acknowledged that the Catholic Church has developed more of the pillars of Western civilisation than any other institution, there is still one other foundational value that the church has nurtured and held as central which, although often hidden to those living in modern Western society, is the basis of our whole civilisation. That is the critical element of freedom.

Within Western society, freedom is the priceless gift that is to be found underpinning all our values, creativity and hopes for our future. Freedom is the great gift of independence from the decisions of others or the decisions of the State.

In the Western World we are usually oblivious to how many components of freedom we are able to exercise in the course of daily life. Australians have considerable freedoms in our speech, with whom we associate, whom to marry, what to read, where to work, how we travel, what to teach our children and which religion to follow. All of these apparently simple freedoms have been hard won and are still not readily available in many societies. The application of Sharia law in Islamic countries or the daily expressions of life in communist or socialist societies radically restricts freedoms we take for granted.

The restrictions to freedom applied in these societies commonly takes the form of reduced individual freedoms. In most cases individual values, knowledge or faith must be adjusted to the demands of a central authority. The outcome of such a societal expression sees loss of economic efficiency and opportunities for growth and a greater degree of unhappiness and depression both for individuals and wider society.

Naturally, the freedoms we enjoy in Western society are also never absolute. A fully functioning individual is also a social one.

We have commitments to families, to schools, to political parties, sporting groups, churches, along with laws of the State and nation. Hopefully, for most of us, these authorities are ones to which we are happy to adhere, and uphold. Nevertheless, the actions of some groups within Western society have become more demanding in their requests for conformity to group regulations. Increasingly, these demands can be seen in workplaces, trade unions, universities, professional sports and most seriously in government and non-government agencies.

The natural attitude of Western civilisation is to resist and seek to restrict the erosion of individual rights to corporate or government authority.

Nevertheless, as societal demands become more complex, increasingly Western civilisation is witnessing demands for greater adherence to outside authorities and the reality that some organisations now compete with each other in seeking to lessen individual moral and value positions.

As Catholics we must be mindful of the rise of institutions restricting our values or beliefs. Government, universities and unions are all defending their rights to be free from outside interference, yet concurrently denying the promotion of Catholic values within their organisations. The "Nanny State" is often depicted as a source of humour as our attention is drawn to the increasing numbers of silly and irrelevant government regulations or corporate behaviours.

Nevertheless, the truth for Australians is that we are assailed with restrictive practices of many difference shades.

Whatever their names: statutory monopolies, exclusive trading regimes or occupational licensing, they are all on the rise. These increasing restrictions are the enemy of the Church and Western civilisation. The growth of government interference in the lives of Australians risks two unnerving results which are known from historical Catholic experience to those living under the depredations of communism.

Firstly, we risk the high likelihood of the erosion of individual motivation and initiative. This can be witnessed in the relatively high rates of start-up businesses in Australia, but the poor rates of growth which show 96.8% unable to grow sufficiently to employ other Australians (Australian government, office of the Chief Economist September 2015).

Secondly, we also know from our lived communist experience that centralisation of political power debilitates government initiative and destroys cultural energy. The truth of communism is that these States were stagnant and without cultural energy for a substantial number of years before their ultimate economic collapse.

Individual freedom and energy to commence a new enterprise or business will not be enough to sustain these initiatives in the face of excessive government interference or regulation. In the same way government provision of economic safety nets are not enough to ensure necessary support for individuals and the ongoing life of a society.

Strategy for Freedom

The current trend towards greater government interference in the lives of individuals requires a readiness and a disposition from the remaining independent associations to resist further incursions on Australian freedoms. Of these independent associations, the Catholic Church is manifestly the most widespread and systematically organised. This does not mean that the Church has the resolve or the fortitude for such an undertaking, even when current inclinations in our society threaten the central doctrines of the Church.

There is an urgent need for a Catholic voice to strengthen those attributes which have given our civilisation and Australian society its resilience and adaptability.

Undoubtedly, the Church must advocate for greater limitations on government, particularly limitations on red tape, excessive taxation and spending. The Church has a central interest in ensuring freedom of speech, of religious freedoms, freedoms of thought within universities and of the greatest freedom to argue and advocate for the spread of its own conception of a just and free society.

At this point of time in Australian history, the Church is no longer advocating for these profound ideas, and risks an existential threat.

Of prime concern for Catholics should be the rediscovery of the key Catholic principle of subsidiarity. This tenet holds that nothing should be done by a larger and more complex organisation which can be done as well by a smaller and single organisation. This principle is a safeguard of limited government and personal freedom. It seriously conflicts with the Government tendency within Western civilisation for ever increasing regulation. Pope John Paul II highlighted this principle in his criticism of the "Social Assistance State" in his 1991 encyclical *Centesimus Annus*. The pope noted that the State emphasis on ever increasing welfare, contradicted the principle of subsidiarity by denying society its responsibilities. For John Paul II this leads to a "loss of human energy and an unfortunate increase in public agencies which are dominated by bureaucratic thinking and less concern for serving their clients".

This central Catholic teaching is totally ignored by the Australian Catholic bishops and leading Catholic aid agencies. In this case, the Church is utterly muddled, forgetting its own history and continuing to affirm state solutions to social problems.

The result is ever increasing welfare, high youth unemployment, and greater numbers of Australians reliant on government assistance in one form or another. This position of the Church is an ongoing disappointment and contributes markedly to its expanding loss of influence and respect in wider Australian society.

Within the wider battle of ideas the Church is also failing to withstand two substantial opponents, both of which seek to remove Catholic ideas from debate within Australian society.

The first group is a cultural-green-left-secularising movement with radically progressive ideas such as same sex marriage, transgender freedoms, pro-abortion rights and doctor assisted suicide. The tactic of labelling critics as homophobic, misogynist or sexist has intimidated the Church to such an extent that it is unwilling to offer alternative views to most of these radical views.

Secondly, the Church is reluctant to criticise the Islamic faith for fear of giving offence. Such anxiety only ensures that the case for Sharia law, which is made on a regular basis, has no counterbalancing religious argument. Australian Catholics should be aware of the debilitating nature of such a legal system, particularly to women, to ideas of personal freedom and to those who seek to exercise freedom of religion. The penalty for Muslims who seek to leave Islam (apostasy) is death. This code is the very antithesis of Catholicism and the Western culture of freedom.

The current debilitated state of Catholicism is largely based on reluctance to celebrate Western culture, the very culture which reflects most positively the Church's values and hopes for the World. Whenever the Church bends to its secular critics, then it risks inertia, lack of energy and ultimately loss of faith.

Ironically, Western culture, is the drawcard for the millions of migrants who seek to enter Western nations fleeing corruption, poverty and lack of freedom. This is the true testament to the value of Western civilisation. What a pity that Australian Catholicism cannot bring itself to affirm the statement of former British Prime Minister David Cameron:

"I am clear about what these values are – and I am equally clear that they should be promoted in every school and to every child in our country. The values I'm talking about – a belief in freedom, tolerance of others, accepting personal and social responsibility, respecting and upholding the rule of law – are the things we should try to live by every day."

Catholicism is an essential force in our civilisation. It is time we all found the courage to again engage with wider Australians.

XII

OPPOSE THE NANNY STATE

The Australian values of mateship, fair go and support for the battler are never more on display than when the nation reacts to the tragedy of bushfires, floods or other disasters.

In fact, the reaction to such adversity is usually followed by a period of introspection on why we can't respond to each other in similar ways in normal circumstances.

Our reaction to human suffering and struggle does give an insight into the wider Catholic understanding of human community. A human community that is fundamentally dependant on each other, where each person is obliged to help others and develop his/or her talents for the benefit of all. In Catholic theology, there is no such thing as a radical individualist. People are by nature designed for community.

Naturally, when we highlight the value of the Australian individual in times of disaster it is also important to think about the kind of society to which we are asking the individual to contribute. Whilst Catholicism is not committed to any forms of government, some forms are considered more likely to develop and foster, the common good. For Catholicism, the common good follows whenever the fundamental rights of individuals are respected and Australians can freely develop their intellectual and religious potential. The Catholic emphasis on the common good implies that people must live in societies associated with freedom and security.

There are serious issues within Australian community life, at the moment, where some governments and organisations are seeking to restrict and remove the right of all Australians to cooperate with each other, and seek their own form of common good.

The common experience for many Australians is now one where over protective and interfering government rules and regulations unduly interfere with personal choice. This is rightly called a "nanny state" as it increasingly treats Australians as children, in ways that restrict freedom but also suggest that cooperation between Australians for their own "common good" is not appropriate and must be limited and ultimately removed.

This development within Australian governments and agencies is essentially uncatholic as it does not apply "just" authority nor encourage the greater goal of the common good.

Indeed, the nanny state works hard to eradicate the individual's power and responsibility to shape their own community life.

The profound Catholic principle of subsidiarity, teaches that what individuals can accomplish by their own initiative and efforts should not be taken from them by a higher authority. A greater and higher social institution must not take over the duties of a subordinate organisation nor deprive it of its competence

(*Catechism of the Catholic Church*, No. 1883-1885). By its very nature, the nanny state removes personal responsibility and increases the scope of law and regulations designed to restrict and undermine personal choice.

Modern Australia is demonstrating, in a number of pronounced ways that nanny state regulations are having a detrimental impact on the ability of Australians to rely on themselves, to join together in community associations to support each other or to work for outcomes they believe in.

Most profoundly, the ability of voluntary community associations to engage in community service, raise funds to support charities, to build their own schools, are all under severe strain in modern Australia.

The evidence for this can be seen in the rapidly decreasing numbers of Australians prepared to volunteer in a whole range of important community associations. Rotary clubs, churches, St John Ambulance, football and cricket clubs, Lort Smith Animal Hospital, country fire associations, golf clubs, St Vincent de Paul, life savers, event volunteers, environmental clean-ups the list is endless of community groups under extreme stress from an unwillingness of people to volunteer.

The ludicrous number of regulations, training and background checks that must be undertaken to participate in Australian community life, is in fact destroying the nature of who we are as a people.

Concurrently, with the erosion of formal volunteering, the numbers of those involved in neighbourhood groups or indeed anyone who actually knows their neighbours is reducing year by year. Charitable giving from the wider Australian community has decreased substantially in the last few years. It is any real surprise that Australians also report dramatic increases of mental illness, of depression, of male suicidality, of loneliness and of disconnection from each other.

Perhaps the French historian and diplomat Alex de Tocqueville best summed up Australian's current situation when he commented on American political changes in 1835 and the seductive promise made by government of security from the cradle to grave. For de Tocqueville this was the key enemy of any civil society.

> "The more the State puts itself in the place of associations, the more particular persons, losing the idea of associating with each other will need to come to their aid. The morality and intelligence of democratic people would risk no few dangers than its business and its industry of the government came to take the place of associations everywhere. Sentiments and ideas renew themselves, the heart is enlarged, the human mind is developed only by the reciprocal action of men upon one another" (Alexis de Tocqueville, *Democracy in America*).

The quantity and idiocy of nanny state control over the lives of Australians is not something in which we can continue our complacency. These forms of micro-management do have an impact on the lives of our children and have certainly restricted the ability of the Catholic Church to connect with and operate community groups. Where are the Catholic sporting clubs, boxing gyms and youth groups for which our church was so noted? Is it really the case that Australian Catholics are reluctant to volunteer to help in such organisations, or is our society giving a stronger message on the diminished value and validity of community life.

Perhaps the most absurd, but in no sense atypical, illustration of the nanny state destroying a young person's dreams can be seen in the treatment of 11 year old Chelsea-lee Downes from Bunbury in Western Australia.

Chelsea-lee with the support of her parents was proposing to open a lemonade stall outside her house, also selling cupcakes and lemon meringue pies. After starting her preparation at 4am and organising furniture and fridge, Chelsea-lee was prohibited from opening by Bunbury City Council officers, who closed her stall before she had a chance to open. The Council's environmental health manager, noted "it is important to seek professional advice in relation to legal requirements" and some of her product ingredients contain custard and cream, again described by the Council as "very high risk products".

Whilst Chelsea-lee's situation may seem pathetic, such episodes are unfortunately repeated day after day across Australia.

Research from the Institute of Public Affairs has highlighted a substantial decrease in new business start-ups, down from 326,000 in 2003/4 to only 284,000 in 2013/4. Notwithstanding Prime Minister Malcolm Turnbull's push to make Australia an innovation hub within Asia, it is plain that for many businesses, senseless bureaucracy is stifling the enthusiasm of Australians for innovative and new business ventures.

Regrettably, in the bigger picture it is younger Australians who are most disadvantaged by nanny state regulations, often deprived of basic childhood experiences enjoyed by earlier generations:

- Belgian Gardens Primary School has banned cartwheels and handstands in their playground, declaring them to be "middle risk level 2" in the Queensland risk management guidelines.

- Mount Martha Primary School (in Victoria) has banned "tiggy" and "chasey games" from the playground, telling parents that this was not an "overreaction to perceived safety issues.

- Southmoor Primary School (in Victoria) has banned the trading of football cards, saying it would spare younger children the "distress of bad trades".

- A Melbourne under 8 cricket association refuses to note individual or team scores or fall of wickets stating that "the only thing that counted was having fun".

The Catholic Church must vigorously oppose nanny state regulations. It must do so not because it wishes to sir-up trouble, but because such rules and regulations are inconsistent with the ideas of a Catholic society. In broad terms, the idea of Catholic society is based on the essence of market freedoms centred on a few fundamental truths.

- Catholic societies allow individuals to make free choice.

- Catholic societies result in individuals pursuing their

own idea of the "good life".

- Catholic societies develop friendships and social contact.
- Catholic societies encourage cooperation and wealth generation.
- Catholic societies encourage behaviour that serves justice.

In all of these fundamental truths the nanny state works as a debilitating or stifling force.

In modern Australia our once vibrant civil society has entered a period of decay, not because of excessive technology but because of the inordinate claims of the State and local councils.

Catholics accept that individuals do live within a complex grouping of institutions to which we owe some loyalty. There is a government, there are economic markets and there is the law, most importantly there is civil society the realm in which the church has had the most bearing and influence. If we do not reclaim our say within this realm, we can no longer expect that Australia will have a free society.

XIII

DEFENDING THE FREE MARKET

In recent years many Australians have become notably sceptical of free markets. In some cases the word "capitalism" has become a byword for perceptions of a society in which we uphold nothing more than a winner-taker-all philosophy.

For some, a fear of free markets is also based on a view of history which sees a small number of chiefs, kings, archbishops, popes or wealthy individuals benefit financially through control of a system which persecutes the poor and ensures that those without resources are not able to obtain them.

The truth of capitalism and free markets is that they have improved the living standards of billions of people in an unprecedented way. There is no other economic system that has been able to realise the world-wide gains for humanity that capitalism and free markets have achieved.

The United Nations Human Development Index (HDI) which ranks countries on economic growth, care of the environment, health and living conditions offers conclusive proof. All of the top twenty nations on the HDI, which includes Australia are characterised by fiscal responsibility, openness to trade, accessible credit and business friendly environments which are low on corruption. Unfortunately, the laggards on HDI success are many South American and African countries, yet the truth surrounding these nations is one of high corruption, excessive taxation, regulatory burdens, poor human rights and weak legal systems.

Significant challenges continue to face South American and African nations, but the solution to poverty reduction is already known: free trade and investments which create jobs and strategies that support entrepreneurs. Coupled with these economic strategies, human flourishing is strengthened by private property rights, free association, the free exchange of ideas and goods all sponsored in a culture of trust and protected by a rule of law. Traditional Catholic social teaching firmly lies within these parameters, not overly exciting, but a proven successful way forward.

All of this, leads us to asking the key question: Why have free markets been so successful". To my view there has been an crucial idea at the heart of free markets which ensures that each new generation will be drawn into free enterprise. This idea is that property rights are identical to personal rights. At the heart of free markets is this foundational idea. If men and women are insecure in their right to buy and own property, then they will be insecure in their human rights. We are not creatures who are only meant to consume, we are meant to create, develop and improve. This idea can be witnessed most profoundly in the difference between the home owner and the tenant. The home owner is empowered to develop his/her own property in ways they see fit. New renovations, additional rooms, improved gardens are all based on the security of personal ownership. On the other hand the tenant is not incentivised to do anything, indeed the tenant may find themselves removed from property, even against their will. The right to property is not absolute, but in societies where this is valued, generally other rights are respected as well.

The history of communism should offer valuable lessons. When society is collectivised and all is owned in common, incentives are removed and energy is lost. When you lose your economic freedom, very soon your other freedoms will be lost as well

Catholicism has also recognised a spiritual and moral dimension to private property, our ability to labour and to use our intelligence to bring into existence a future that did not previously exist. The building of a beautiful cathedral or the creation of art, along with a medical discovery, the development of better food supplies or the completion of a new garden are all aspects of human beings applying thoughtful stewardship to our possessions and our property.

These developments can only be undertaken if we have a view of "things" which sees them as not just to be consumed. In the Catholic view "things" do more than help us survive, they are essential to our reasoning and creative abilities. The Church rightly recognises that our ability to apply our intelligence to possessions and ideas is central to our creativity, our futures and our stewardship of what we own. For Catholicism, property rights is another fundamental human right, not granted to us by the State but imbedded in our nature and existence.

Throughout its history the Catholic Church has resisted and opposed all types of governments that have restricted property rights in the recognition that such actions are also an attack on religious freedom. When private property is not secure the church itself will be vulnerable.

This tension can be seen in the Catholic aversion to many historical kings, dictators or political systems. On the surface, there is not much in common between Henry VIII, fascism, communism, socialism or Islamic governance except they all have philosophical opposition to private ownership and control of property, unless you belong to a certain, class ethic group or political faction.

Catholicism has learnt through history that it is hard to uphold human rights in the absence of property rights. We can see this clearly in the right to free speech. Many dictators and oppressive regimes will champion the notion of free speech, yet, if their citizens are unable to publish privately, own a newspaper or TV station or own or read certain types of literature, then in what sense do they really have free speech?

It is not just deplorable regimes like Castro's Cuba, or Stalin's Russia that claim free speech rights or democracy and ensure the opposite. Democratic governments can also display these tendencies. In 2012 the Obama Administration in the United States, required Catholic hospitals, homes and care institutions to ensure abortion services, sterilization and contraception facilities were available through their organisations in contempt of Catholic moral opposition to such practices.

Freedom of religion, independence of conscience or even operating your own institutions in the way you see fit is increasingly difficult if you are financially dependent on the State. This is the great dilemma facing the Australian Catholic Church in regards to its schools and hospitals, all heavily funded by government. The example of political control in the United States where freedom of religion is loudly proclaimed but ignored in the provision of services does reflect changes occurring in Western societies.

It is important that the Australian Catholic Church takes notice and recognises that if it will not defend free markets which support religious freedom, Australian governments will increasingly undertake decisions which override religious freedoms. The Andrews government in Victoria has already done this with its abortion laws, its removal of religious education in State Schools, its "safe school program", which supports alternative sexuality and lifestyles and its repeated attempts to legislate for doctor assisted suicide.

These are all issues that are fundamentally about religious freedom and the central place of private institutions in society. Should we look to government to provide for every dimension of a citizen's life with society? Or is there a role in the private sector for organisations that pursue their own values and goals, provided charitable work and encourage independence in educational, medical, economic and moral formation. This has always been the essential position of the Catholic Church within Australia. In recent years however, the Church has pulled back from the support of such positions and indeed encouraged greater regulation, and involvement of the State in the lives of Australians, notably in welfare provision, indigenous issues and refugee matters. In this new socialist manifestation of the church, Australian Catholicism is encouraging severe restrictions to its own life, independence and influence in Australian Society.

The central delusion of all forms of communism and socialism is the belief that an economy can be based on collective ownership. History loudly proclaims this idea as an utter failure, in any culture, geographic area or time frame. It is also time the church in Australia proclaimed this failure as well. With private ownership, within free markets, individuals undertake the proper task of stewardship responsibility – caring for what belongs to them. This is a central Catholic idea because it is central to the free individual created in the image of God.

XIV

MAKE A GENUINE DIFFERENCE TO THE POOR

For many years in one of Melbourne's inner city parishes, a popular priest operated a daily open house lunch where a regular number of local men attended faithfully, ate food, watched TV, drank coffee, read newspapers and generally hung-out. When I inquired as to the future prospects of these men I was told by the priest "oh they can't do anything, they are the survivors of the 1980's drug wars".

Yet, as I increasingly engaged with these men I could see that few of them had lost their intellectual abilities, their reading and writing was strong and their conversational opinions were logical and vigorously argued. At no stage did any of them contribute financially to their meals nor do any work around the parish, despite their being a significantly overgrown garden that need substantial attention.

After witnessing this "groundhog" day for a period I concluded that indeed, this particular parish was doing nothing to provide for the dignity or spirit of these men. Rather, by addressing only a narrow set of needs, it was keeping them in poverty despite claiming they were serving the poor. This parish had really given up on these men presuming they had nothing to offer, they were seen as little more than mouths to feed not as human beings with creativity, energy and capabilities.

This is a difficult reality for many Catholic parishes to recognise: much of what we do is allowing people to survive but not much else. In many of our programs and initiatives we have forgotten about the key way that people escape poverty: They get a job!

The data is incontrovertible, when individuals or indeed nations pursue work and free enterprise, the economy develops and large numbers of people rise out of poverty.

On a national level, we can see this clearly in the examples of North and South Korea. In the South, the government is far more supportive of basic human rights and free enterprise and has a deeper understanding of the key components of human dignity, personal growth and the spirituality of freedom. These things drive human achievement and fulfilment. In Catholic language they allow us to be co-creators with God, in our personal and national futures. In more common language, it is a job that leads to well-being and security.

In the North, however we see government opposed to economic, political and religious freedom, for that matter freedom of any kind. This situation breeds poverty, as it blocks basic human creativity, hopes and abilities.

It may be that this is an offensive suggestion, but are we really any difference to North Koreans if our aid and welfare does not drive people to improve themselves, move out of poverty and pursue a future of their own self-determination? Authentic Catholic charity cannot be about feeding people for the next forty years, it must be about engaging with them in enterprise, getting a job and embarking on their own future. Unfortunately, in some parts of the Catholic Church there is a primitive view that "capitalism" and "free-markets" are dirty words and that given a chance large business enterprises will always look to "rip-off" the little person. We need to rid ourselves of this false idea.

In a market economy, such as Australia where the rule of law is enforced businesses don't thrive by robbing others. It is their foresight in anticipating the needs of consumers and providing quality goods at affordable prices that ensures success. In only fifty years, South Korean companies such as Samsung, Hyundai, Kia, Hanva and LG have all become major export companies throughout the World. The obvious question is why can't Australia? This is an objective that Australian Catholics should be supporting – enterprise produces jobs, which in turn produces creative, cooperative, mentally healthy individuals more likely to engage in and sustain family and community life.

Catholic clergy are especially prone to a prejudice against business and enterprise. The reality is that many priests support systems of redistribution. After all this is the way we operate our parishes. We send around the plate and then redistribute these funds to pay bills or operate programs. The difficulty with this system is that clergy do not ask themselves where the money comes from in the first place! It comes from the work and enterprise of the parishioners! Most clergy are not generators of funds or engaged in enterprise activity. Correctly, they are not called to do this. Nevertheless, those who do not generate wealth, get paid and live at parish expense (whether they do a good job or not) should not be suggesting that redistribution from government to welfare agencies is the only method available to Australians to reduce poverty and encourage more people into work. Catholicism is a religion of work not welfare. We degrade people and betray our fundamental Catholic nature when we imagine that supporting people in welfare has contributed something to their well-being. It has not.

In Genesis, humanity is described as being made in the image of God. This likeness is also stipulated by God as a creative process, "be faithful and multiply". Naturally, our creativity is seen in the procreation of children, yet the human creative capacity is not limited to this. The great gift of creativity is to be extended to all that we do, it is given to us to provide for ourselves, our families and for others. In this way we live in the image of God.

The great Pope John Paul II was very prescient when he recognised that "work is not just a mere necessity, but must be considered a real vocation" (Monterrey Mexico 1979). The essential nature of work as being central to the Gospel was consistently highlighted in John Paul II's thoughts and understandings.

"Work is good for us. Through work we not only transform

nature, adapting it to our needs, but we also achieve fulfilment as human beings and indeed become more fully human" (Monterey, California 1897).

"I come to announce the Gospel of work" (Barcelona, Spain 1982).

"It must be said over and over again that work is for man, not man for work ... the worker is always more important than profit and machines" (Sydney, Australia 1986).

"The son of God became man and worked with human hands...... So we know, not only by reason alone but through revelation, that through their work people share in God's creative work. We continue it and, in a sense, perfect it by our own work, our toil, by daily effort to wrest a livelihood from the earth, or from the sea, or by applying energy to the many difference processes of production ... indeed we Christians are convinced that the achievements of the human race – in art, science, culture and technology – are a sign of God's greatness and the flourishing of God's mysterious design" (Busan, Sth Korea 1984).

The economic and moral issues that we face today in modern Australian are connected. Employment for those in need may seem to be merely an economic matter, nevertheless for Catholicism it is much deeper. The societies and nations that have found ways of releasing creativity through economic freedom, have lifted millions from poverty. Work is what is needed, creative, entrepreneurial and free. This is not just good for the poor but lies at the very heart of Catholicism itself.

For Consideration

- Why is the Catholic Church in Australia not involved in enterprise creation at the level of each diocese and each parish? Imagine the possibilities for new employment in local communities

- The Catholic Church has excellent opportunities to develop and support specific options for the training and preparation of work of young Australians. One success story already exists: fatherjamesgrantfoundation.org.

XV

CONTESTING SHARIA LAW

There is broad Muslim community support for aspects of Sharia law to be adopted in Australia. Two of Australia's most prominent Muslims, Keysar Trad, President of the Islamic Friendship Association of Australia and Zachariah Matthews, President of the Australian Islamic Mission have called for aspects of Sharia law to run parallel to Western Common Law. Both men noted that adopting Sharia marital and Inheritance law would be an advantage for Australian Muslims, as currently the Australian Government does not recognise divorce documents made by Imams, the mosque and community leaders. Currently, the Australian Muslim population is around 340,000 or 1.7% of the population.

These calls for the implementation of Sharia, whether in full or part are now a common feature of Islamic communities living within Western nations. Australia is no different in this regard.

Nevertheless, there is much that can be learned from the experience of Muslim presence in other Western States, particularly the European Union.

- Sharia tribunals operate in the United Kingdom. These Tribunals openly defend a man's "right" to use violence against his wife. In many parts of the UK and Denmark "Sharia controlled zones" enforce Sharia laws, particularly in relation to female dress codes and consumption of alcohol.

- Within areas in which these tribunals operate, violence against wives and honour violence has increased. Homosexual couples and Jewish groups report dramatically raised levels of harassment and intimidation.

- Universities and local councils are pressured into providing gender segregated swimming pools and additional recreational facilities for the exclusive use of Muslim women (also in Australia)

- Workplaces are being forced to provide Islamic prayer rooms and give Muslim workers time off to pray.

There are currently extensive debates across Europe, the USA and Canada concerning the compatibility of Sharia law with Western law and the rights of individuals, extensively supported and to a large extent developed by Western Catholicism.

Sharia law itself is based on the principles found in the Koran, the Sira and Hadith. These texts acknowledge that there is and can be, no common principles between Western law and Sharia.

Under Sharia law there is no freedom of religion. Jews and Christians who continue to disbelieve and do not convert to Islam will go to hell. "The unbelievers of the people of the book and the idolaters shall be in the fire of Hell, therein dwelling forever, those are the worst of creatures" (Q98.6) Additionally, Muslims consider themselves superior to other peoples, and their role is to instruct others on the truth. In contrast most Jews and Christians are wrongdoers. "You are the best nation ever brought forth to men, bidding to honour, and forbidding dishonour. Some of the people of the book are believers, but most of them are ungodly" (Q.3. 110).

Finally, freedom of religion is denied, as Islam's destiny is to rule over all religions "It is Allah who has sent his messenger, with the guidance and the religion of truth. Allah will ensure to triumph over every religion" (Q 48.28).

There is a vast chasm between the fundamental position of Catholicism which views humans as God's partners, made in his image and a divine character expressed most strongly in Philippians 2, 6-8, "who, being in very nature God, did not consider equality with God as something to be used to his own advantage, rather, he made himself nothing by taking the very nature of a servant being made in human likeness. And being found in the appearance as a man he humbled himself by becoming obedient to death – even death on a cross". Under Sharia law, the notion of God who engages freely with humans, considers them his partners, gives them free will and encourages them to love him in freedom is utterly absent.

Under Sharia law there is no essential concept of human freedom, either granted by God or encouraged as a vital concept in human life.

Within Sharia there is no freedom of speech, nor freedom of thought, subsequently there is no freedom of the press and no freedom of artistic expression.

Of most serious concern, Sharia discriminates heavily against certain classes of people, notably non-Muslims who are permanently classified as second class citizens and women for whom there is no equality either in general law or within family precepts. Muslims also have a significant disregard for non-Islamic law, contending that all forms of government must be ruled by Sharia principles.

Possibly the best known difficulties associated with Sharia law concern the treatment of women, "Allah has made men superior to women because men spend their wealth to support them. Therefore virtuous women are obedient and they are to guard their unseen parts as Allah has guarded them. As for women whom you fear will rebel, admonish them first, and then send them to a separate bed, and then beat them" (Q 4.34). The Islamic doctrine towards women underlines a deep suspicion, which asserts that women are fundamentally untrustworthy both in their nature, who have the potential to tempt men into poor behaviour, but also in their lukewarm devotion to Islam, which is often lacking. The reality for women under Sharia law is that they do not have equitable status.

"Mohammad asked, Is not the value of a women's eye witness testimony half that of a man. A woman said, yes it is, Mohammad said, this is because a woman's mind is deficient" (Bukhari 3 48,862).

Mohammad, when speaking to a group of women, noted that most of the people in Hell are women. The group of women asked, why is that? "He answered, you swear too much, and you show no gratitude to your husbands. I have never come across anyone more lacking in intelligence, or ignorant of their religion than women. A careful and intelligent man could be misled by many of you". They responded, what exactly are we lacking in intelligence or faith? Mohammad said, "Is it not true that the testimony of one man is equal to the testimony of two women". After they affirmed that it was true, Mohammad said, "That illustrates that women are lacking in intelligence. Is it also not true that women may not pray nor fast during their menstrual cycle"? They said that this was also true. Mohammad then said, "That illustrates that women are lacking in their religion".

Sharia law is also highly discriminatory to women within the family context. It is lawful for a freeborn Muslim to marry up to four women, conjugal rights are obligatory for women upon male request and the central contribution a woman makes in the home is not companionship or partnership with the husband but her sexuality.

"Mohammad said, The marriage vow most rightly expected to be obeyed is the husband's right to enjoy the wife's vagina" (Bukhari 7, 82 81). Islamic family law also shapes two other highly contentious issues of Islamic behaviour, under age marriage and female circumcision. Mohammad when he was aged 51 proposed marriage to Aisha who was then only six years old. Whilst some

Islamic scholars will suggest that consummation of marriage cannot have taken place until the onset of menstruation, the actions of Mohammad have established that such marriages are acceptable for all Muslims and during any historical period. The Bukhari hadith gives wider content: "When Mohammad asked Abu Bakr for Aisha's hand in marriage. Abu replied, 'but I am your brother, Mohammad said,' you are only my brother in Allah's religion and his book, so it is lawful for me to marry her" (Bukhari, 7.62,18).

The classic Sharia law text is entitled the "Reliance of the Traveller". Here the position of Sharia regarding female circumcision is made clear: "Circumcision is obligatory by cutting off the piece of skin on the glans of the penis for the male, but circumcision of the female is by cutting off the clitoris" (Reliance of the Traveller e, 4.3).

The advent of Islamic immigration into Australia has also brought into sharper focus relationships between Muslim and non-Muslim not only in Australia, but throughout the world.

The Islamic word for non-Muslim is "kafir" and is usually translated as unbeliever, yet within Quaranic and Hadith context the word has a much deeper meaning. Originally, the word meant concealer, that is someone who conceals the truth of Islam from others. Naturally, such kafirs within the Quran are held in contempt, and it is permissible to deceive them to mock them, to torture and to enslave them.

The wider problem for Christians and Jews is that Islam has its own definition for these faiths which are not premised on how these faiths see themselves. Christianity for example is only legitimate if Christians acknowledge that there is no trinity, that Jesus was only a man, was not crucified, not resurrected and upon his return will establish Sharia law. The Islamic view of Judaism insists that all true Jews must acknowledge that Mohammad is the final prophet for Judaism and supersedes all prophets in Jewish scriptures.

"Make war on those who have received the scriptures, but do not believe in Allah or in the last day. They do not forbid what Allah and his messenger have forbidden. The Christian and Jews do not follow the religion of truth until they submit and pay the tax and are humiliated" (Quran 9:29).

"Then the Lord spoke to his angels and said 'I will be with you and give strength to the believers. I will send terror into the kafirs hearts, cut of their heads and even the tips of their fingers'" (Quran 8:12).

"Kafirs will be cursed, and whenever they are found, they will be seized and murdered. It was Allah's same practice with those who came before them, and you will find no change in Allah's ways" (Quran 33:60).

Regrettably, Sharia law has no concept of equality of people nor equality of religion. Its underlying principle is that all people and ideas must submit to Islam. This has subsequently ensured that many Muslims see kafirs as the enemy, simply for not being Muslims. These arbitrary and absolute theological views also have made certain that violence is intimately wrapped up in Quranic teaching. Peace for non-Muslims comes only with submission to Islam. "Mohammad said "I have been ordered to wage war against mankind until they accept that there is no God but Allah and that they believe I am his prophet and accept all revelations spoken through me" (Muslim 001, 0031).

"To battle kafirs in Jihad for one day is greater than the entire earth and everything on it" (Bukhari 4. 52.142).

Coupled with this view of non-Muslims found in the Koran and Hadith, there is an additional set of Sharia rules governing the behaviour of non-Muslims who live in Islamic nations. These are known as Dhimmi laws. In the modern framework these rules are rarely expressed openly, but exist in practice. Of notable concern is the ongoing situation of Coptic Christians in Egypt. Within Egypt, restrictions exist on the construction of new churches and those destroyed in acts of violence. Young Coptic Christians are often rejected in application for university and the situation of those who have converted from Islam to Christianity remains dire.

In a 2010 Pew research found that 84% of Egyptian Muslims believe those who leave Islam should be killed. There are dozens of cases in Egypt of Muslims apostatising to Christianity only to be attacked by families, neighbours, colleagues or just gangs of thugs.

Egyptian courts can be just as brutal, regularly failing to uphold basic human rights. In February 2009, Maher Al-Gohary tried to officially convert to Christianity, only to be accused of apostatising, prosecutors calling for the death penalty. As Maher himself has reflected.

"Our rights in Egypt, as Christians or converts, are less than the rights of animals. We are deprived of social and civil rights, deprived of our inheritance and left to the fundamentalists to be killed. Nobody bothers to investigate or care about us".

Attacks on Christians and converts are on the rise throughout the Islamic world. This unfortunately demonstrates unwavering persistence of Muslims – regardless of nationality, race, ethnicity or language to continually persecute the lives of Christians or converts. At the heart of this persecution is Sharia law. The idea of freedom of religion and thought is impossible under Sharia law. All thought must be submitted to the Koran and Sharia. The only tolerance is for Islam. The Catholic Church in Australia has been disgraceful and cowardly in its failure to highlight the realities for Christians across the world of Islam. There has not been a single statement of significance from any diocese or bishops, either parish communities or to the wider Australian community in regard to the rampant persecution of Christians throughout the world. This is a shameful situation which embarrasses all Catholics and calls into question the faith of Australian Catholics, given we maintain the right to worship in peace, but will do nothing to ensure other Christians enjoy similar rights.

Middle Eastern Christianity is under severe stress, its churches are destroyed and Muslim supremacists are trying to convert, subjugate or kill Christians. The Australian media observers the suffering of Christians and suggests that persecutions are the result of economic inequalities.

The strength and long term resilience of the Australian Catholic Church rests on its ability to stand up for its beliefs, at home and abroad. At the moment the character of Australian Catholics and leadership would appear to be lacking.

XVI

RECLAIM THE WORKPLACE

The importance of work for human redemption is powerfully emphasised in the teachings of Jesus. Pope John Paul II himself has referred to Jesus as "the man of work" (Trujillo, 1985) who from his earliest days worked at the side of Joseph. A common early description of Jesus notes that he is "the carpenter's son". For John Paul II "this work of the Son of God, constitutes the first and fundamental Gospel, the Gospel of work" (Trujillo, 1985).

The important parable of the talents (Matthew 25: 14-25) depicts a master placing his servants in charge of his goods while away on a trip. Upon his return he evaluates his servants according to their ability to make wise investments that generated a profit. It is apparent that the master expected an increase of his wealth during his absence. He determines two servants to have been "faithful" to his wishes and rewards their actions. For a third hesitant servant who does not invest his "talent", he commits him to the punishment of "outer darkness" in a place with weeping and gnashing of teeth.

John Paul II accurately acknowledges that these first two examples offer a pattern for the desirability and benefit of work.

The mission that God entrusts to each of his followers is to double the value of each one's talents. For those who are fainthearted or refuse to work, the one talent that is wasted in inactivity ensures that other talents will be wasted as well. In this parable the divine judgement depends heavily on our understanding the value and importance of work and of committing to its growth and challenges. On the other hand, the "wasting of one's talent" brings a diminishing of future talents and ultimate atrophy.

In this way, work is the fundamental social justice issue and is central to understanding all other human problems. The church certainly wants to help the poor, not just in the economic sphere, but in the cultural and moral spheres as well. The poor person is not only someone who lack material goods but in the Christian understanding is someone who is immersed in sin, be that self-indulgence, indifference to others, or a refusal to act on God-given gifts to be used for the benefit of all. In the Catholic conception of society, the church continues to affirm the sacred dignity of each person and therefore the dignity of every worker.

As John Paul II notes:

> "This dignity corresponds to a series of fundamental rights. The right to have a job, a job in order to live, to be able to fulfil oneself as a person, to provide bread for one's family. A job that enriches society, a job that must be carried out in conditions worthy of a person and a job that does not damage either physical health or moral integrity" (Trujillo, 1985).

The centrality of social justice is work, along with the building of a more just society, this depends totally on the union of entrepreneurs and workers. Without such a unity in work there can be no fulfilment of individual human dignity or society.

In recent years the Australian Catholic Church has lost interest and influence in this core Catholic understanding of the centrality of work issues to Australian society. The Church has a poor comprehension and appreciation of the role of business to Australian economic health or the vital place that entrepreneurs and small businesses have within it. The Church no longer has significant relationships with any group of unionists within Australia. In recent years the Catholic Bishops conference has produced statements on social justice for aging Australians, the need to strengthen indigenous families, the threats to marriage and human trafficking. All of these are worthwhile issues for a Catholic voice within Australia, but they are not fulfilling what John Paul II referred to as the key Catholic perception.

> "The Church is convinced that work is a fundamental dimension of human existence on earth ... the Church considers it her duty to speak out on work ... It is her particular duty to form a spirituality of work which will help all people to come closer, through work, to God ... This Christian spirituality of work should be a heritage shared by all" (*Laborem Exercens*, 1981).

The Australian Catholic Church's failure to engage with work questions and concerns, has left the church seriously disconnected from mainstream Australian life and unable to lead or guide the Australian community in engagement with Catholic knowledge and wisdom. By investing its energy in non-important social issues, such as refugees, indigenous culture, and increasing welfare transfers, the modern church has ensured its status as a minor and peripheral participant in Australian life.

What can the Catholic Church do?

Australia's most serious ongoing problem is the lack of good jobs. That is full-time jobs that allow Australians to expand their talents and advance our society in ways that help others to flourish. Despite the determination of Catholic leaders to continuously promote issues like refugees, indigenous integration and higher rates of unemployment benefit, these remain nowhere near our most critical issues. Runaway government spending is a problem, rising health costs are disturbing, terrorism will remain a global difficulty into the foreseeable future, but the core issue above all others, is getting and maintaining a decent job. The most critical subset of Australia's unemployment crisis is the situation affecting young Australians whose unemployment rate is officially judged at 13%, but most likely runs much higher.

Work goes to the heart of what it means to be a functioning Catholic. If you cannot find and hold a job, in what sense is marriage a viable option, in what sense is purchasing a home conceivable, in what sense is commencing a family likely, and in what sense is persevering in the faith aspiring?

All these Catholic "goods" are premised on having and holding a job.

Pope John Paul II understands this, the magisterium of the

Church and tradition teaches this, all begging the question "why has the Australian church forgotten a foundational ministry of faith"?

We do in Australia know a great deal about unemployment. It is long established that people out of work for periods of more than 12 months report deteriorating health consequences. They suffer from fractured sleep, are more likely to be depressed, have increased levels of anger and experience a loss of friendship and family networks – all resulting in greater loneliness and sense of disconnection.

Critically, individuals who endure long periods of unemployment experience discontinuity with their communities which can last for many decades or may never be restored. This can be seen in the low levels of volunteerism, generally witnessed in long-term unemployed individuals. Unemployment makes changes in our social relationships, our commitment to our communities, our pride in our nation or State, but most importantly in our sense of self.

Clearly, having a job is worth more than financial benefits, particularly if you derive a sense of mission and purpose from work. Conversely being unemployed for any more than a few months has severe impacts on all dimensions of human life.

The world of work in modern Australia is critically linked to small businesses and local entrepreneurs. Small business accounts for nearly 50% of private industry sector employment and contribute 1/3 of private sector added value (Treasury ABS 2013).

The bulk of these business initiatives are in the service sector (84.4%) and deal directly with fellow Australians in their local and regional areas.

Accordingly, Australian Catholics must recognise that the most important work and employment solutions are local. Support for Australian small business must be concentrated on local job creation, training business leaders and encouraging entrepreneurs. Why are Australian Catholics not involved in owning and operating local business initiatives? Why are we not focused on local job creation, on career development and on enhancing business leadership? The Catholic Church has a responsibility to fund, create and develop new businesses that employ people and give them the expertise to be the most creative and talented they can be. As a consequence of our failure to develop these employment initiatives, we are naturally viewed as disinterested in this core area of concern with Australia. Without skin in the game we remain fringe dwellers with few insights or accurate appraisals of how to really develop Australian economic life.

Another important understanding for the Church to absorb is that the global and Australian economy is desperate for knowledge workers. Certainly, traditional jobs in some industries will still be needed, but clothing manufacturing, for example, cannot be a leading job strategy. In an important new way, the Church must be in constant engagement with new local entrepreneurs, supporting individual initiative, supporting meritocracy and greater competition in free markets. Australian Catholicism is currently severely weakened in its dealings with wider Australia. As it has no connections and offers no support to young business enterprise and yet constantly calls for increased government regulation in many areas of Australian life. Australian Catholicism must do better in this area. It is the lifeblood of the Australian community and we are absent from this important field. It is also critical that Catholicism understands, as Pope John Paul II did, that economic strength originates in the heart and minds of individuals, not government.

Government has a vital role to play in many areas of our national life, but no Australian government has ever ignited a sustainable economic boom nor has it ever produced quality long-term employment.

A particular role for the Church could be in mentoring, advising, encouraging and financially engaging with business at critical moments. This is the essential aspect of creating new jobs. Australia has many talented entrepreneurs but we lack the organisation capable of supporting innovation and encouraging risk.

This is my great personal issue with Australian Catholicism at the moment. We behave like a socialist government enterprise, we are afraid of change, we are afraid of losses, both reputational and financial and the consequence has been that we are flabby, complacent and with nothing new to offer.

My argument is simple: The world of work is the most important dimension of Australian life: no economy, no future. Australian governments have no idea how to create work. It is time for Australian Catholics with a significant national network to fill the gap. It might make a difference the way Australians see us and we see ourselves, but it requires courage!

XVII

STAND UP FOR PERSECUTED CHRISTIANS

There is no doubt that Christians are the most persecuted group of people in the world. It is also unquestionable that this persecution is largely ignored both by secular Western media and to our great shame by Australian Catholics.

The furious reaction that accompanied media investigations into Abu Ghraib, Guantanamo Bay and alleged injustices to Australian David Hicks have not been forthcoming over the appalling violation of human rights and murder metered out to Christians across the globe.

Christianity today can be found in most countries, but it is often the case that Catholics and other denominations form minorities in many regions. Additionally, these Christian communities are from non-white racial groups, often ethnic minorities and contain a higher percentage of women. This reality sees many of these communities struggling to integrate locally, with majorities who sometimes treat them as deserving of discrimination and aggressive conversion tactics. The abduction and forced conversion of many Christian girls has reached widespread proportions in some regions.

The wretched treatment of minority Christians is a significant barometer for the health of human rights and the rule of law in many Muslim majority nations, along with Marxist and left wing secular states. This does not auger well for the state of human rights.

All this forces on examination as to why secular western media outlets are completely indifferent to reporting any aspects of this global Christian persecution. No clear answer is readily available except perhaps to highlight the severe anti-Christian stereotypes portrayed in Western education, movies and historical revisionism. All these portrayals see Christians as the initiators of the crusades, responsible for various historical inquisitions and within Western nations the widespread protection and cover-up of vile and repulsive clergy abuse against children entrusted to the care of the Church. The reality is that Western secular media has given up on Catholicism. In their view, Catholics are without integrity. Whilst Australian Catholics can be disappointed in such crude caricatures of the faith, the aggression of the secular media is in some ways broadly understandable, the silence of the Australian church is not.

This silence is timid and demonstrates a church self-focused, and out of touch with its own faithful base, but more broadly with the entire Australian community. The Catholic faithful want the Church to stand up for what it believes in, but this cannot be a feel good, meet my needs, self-improvement church. Such messages are without power and without the ability to change Australian society.

For Catholics there is a special obligation to come to the aid of our suffering brothers and sisters. We are all one in Christ through baptism. Suffering in any part of Christ's body is suffering in all. The question for Australian Catholics is: does this mean anything or is it just another feel good phrase?

The extent of the persecution

The insecure nature of Christian freedom within Islamic nations is rooted in the biased application of Sharia law both in countries that fully implement its dictates or those that are influenced by it. Sharia denies freedom to Christians in three distinct ways. Firstly, new Christians suffer reprisals against themselves and their families if they seek to convert to Christianity from Islam. Apostasy from Islam is considered a reprehensible crime, punishments are always severe and include execution. These apostasy laws in effect ban freedom of religion.

Sharia also enforces blasphemy laws which are often used to restrict Christians from spreading their faith or even verbally criticising Islam "those who abuse Allah and his messenger – Allah has cursed them in this world and the hereafter and prepared for them a humiliating punishment" (Quran 33:57). "The penalty for those who wage war against Allah and his messenger (verbal or physical) and strive upon earth to cause mischief is none but that they be killed or crucified or that their hands and feet be cut off from opposite sides or that they be exiled from the land" (Quran 5:33). Blasphemy laws in Sharia, in reality constrains freedom of thought and ensures a climate of permanent fear for Christian communities living within Sharia jurisdictions.

Finally, Sharia prohibits freedom of speech, in that it restrains proselytism or preaching to Muslims on any of the fundamental doctrines of the Catholic faith, the divinity of Christ, the resurrection and the trinity – all doctrines that contradict Muhammad's teachings. In most Islamic states, Catholics are forbidden to display bibles around Muslims who may be seduced into doubt or temptation. They are not to make Christianity appealing and perhaps most shockingly they are prohibited from thwarting Christians from converting to Islam.

Islamic abuse of Christians under Sharia law is undoubtedly the largest source of persecution against Christians in today's world.

The situation of the world's Christians has been deteriorating over a long period of time. We should remind ourselves that more Christians have died for their faith in the last century than in the previous nineteen put together. In 2016, 90,000 Christians were murdered for their faith: that is one killed every six minutes. It is important to realise that persecution of Christians is not exclusively related to Islamic Sharia law, although this is where most persecution is found. The most aggressive persecutor of Christians is North Korea and has been so for around seventy years. Since 1948 it is estimated that more than 3m Christians have been put to death. Currently, between 30-70,000 are incarcerated in political prisons, where starvation, torture and murder are the norm.

Undoubtedly, the Kim dynasty now in its third generation, has deified its political system to a point where, like Islam they are unable to tolerate other theological views.

The fate of Iraq and Syria, both formerly ancient Christian heartlands, is of major concern as Christianity may be on the verge of extinction. In Iraq, a population of one million in 2003 has been reduced to around 275,000. In Syria the reduction has been from 1.5 million to less than 500,000. Most of these have been displaced and now exist as camp refugees in unwelcoming Islamic countries like Turkey and Jordan.

Nigeria is a country of over 190 million people, with slightly more than half being Muslim and dominant in the north, the remainder are Christian and a majority in the south. Christians in central and northern Nigeria face persecution from two armed militias: Boko Harum in the north, which claims to have destroyed over 900 churches and Fulani in the central region, noted for attaching Christian villages and destroying crops. Over 30,000 Christians have been murdered by these two groups in the last 15 years. The central government has no control over these regions.

Egypt's ten million Coptic Christians who make up 10% of the population have endured persecution for over 1400 years. They are still treated as second class citizens and are forced to list their religion on national ID cards which facilitates discrimination against them. The government acts as an ally for the Muslim population, enforcing subtle persecution, for example, restrictions on buildings or renovation of churches is common with around fifty churches currently forbidden to rebuild. Nevertheless the government opens ten new mosques per week, and protects them from planning restrictions.

Although Egypt purports to be a moderate Islamic country, in reality it continues to oppress its Christian population and intentionally keep them as a permanent underclass. Attacks on Christian homes and businesses are common. Christian women are regularly abducted, raped, forcibly married and converted. Police often ignore investigations into such crimes.

In recent years the bombing of Coptic churches has risen sharply. In December 2016, 25 people were killed and hundreds injured at St Marks Coptic cathedral in Cairo. No perpetrators have been arrested. Israel condemned "these reprehensible attacks on Coptic Christians". No Australian Catholic bishop made such a condemnation.

Saudi Arabia, an ultra-conservative Islamic country is the most wealthy and religiously influential nation in the Middle East. Only Sunni Islam may be practised publically; any Saudi converting to another religion is guilty of apostasy, punishable by death. Christian residents are subjected to imprisonment and deportation if caught meeting together. Whilst publically opposed to Islamic terrorism, from within its own fundamentalist Wahhabi theology, hundreds of extremist groups have emerged. Saudi Arabia invests billions of dollars in building mosques and schools throughout the world. In India alone between 2011-1013 25,000 Saudi trained clerics arrived, bringing over $250 million to build mosques and schools. Australia is also subjected to similar initiatives with many new mosques in Australia happy to receive Saudi funding. Australian Catholics and Christians, like the rest of the Western world have not expressed concern over such developments.

The Australian Catholic Church has been very poor in its support for persecuted Christians. This is an issue of great shame for all Australian Catholics.

If you are interested in understanding or supporting the situation for persecuted Christians, International Christian concern, is an interdenominational organisation with significant online news and articles. You can subscribe to receive its free publications at icc@persecution.org.

XVIII

WHAT TO DO ABOUT ROBOTS

Throughout the nineteenth and twentieth centuries, fears have regularly been expressed that machines would eventually destroy a major proportion of human labour, leading to long-term unemployment. So far, this has not happened, indeed improvements in technology have actually driven us towards a more prosperous society. Nevertheless, the history of computing suggests that once operating systems have been merged with easy to use programming, then an explosion of software is sure to follow. There is no doubt that something similar is poised to happen in the field of robotics. We already see a dramatic enhancement of robotics in factory automation. Robots work continuously, don't get sick, suffer from stress or require superannunation payments. They are becoming easier to re-engineer for new tasks and do not incur social media protests over working conditions or high suicide rates caused by long work demands. Increasingly, global companies are equating profitability and sometimes just survival with "engineering the labour out of the product" (Barney Jopson, *American Financial Times*, 27 June 2013).

Disruption in working practices has never been absent from modern economics, but Western nations are undoubtedly about to experience another serious upheaval.

In Australia, as in most other Western nations, a majority of workers are now found in the service industries. The stress to workers in these fields can already be seen with the advent of ATM's and self-service supermarket check-out lanes. This disruption in the service industries is alive and well, machines already exist that can make over 360 speciality hamburgers per hour. Imagine the disruption to the 90,000 Australians who work at McDonalds alone, when such machines enter workplaces. Traditionally, low wages, few benefits and high employment turnover have made fast food outlets the employer of first and last resort for Australians with low education, who are unable to find better employment options. My own Foundation www.fatherjamesgrantfoundation.org works actively with disengaged and demotivated young Australians to open the possibility of their first job. Not surprisingly entry level work gets harder and harder to find or retain as more and more companies casualise such workers.

There are still jobs in security, food and beverage, hotels, gaming and retailers, but employment in these sectors are very much under threat. The strongest growth in Australia over the next 10 years is expected to come in the health sector, most notably aged care, nursing and alternative therapies. As the Australian population ages there may well be significant growth in these fields, nevertheless disruption is never far behind. We already see mobile phones providing shop, scan, pay or offering virtual assistance in some retail settings. How long before the checkout itself is gone and groceries loaded robotically into your car?

The responce to continued automation and its effects on jobs and incomes must become a central Catholic question, yet we do no research, don't engage with business or workers and have nothing to say in this vital moral space. The lack of thought from the Church is alarming.

Nevertheless, an obvious moral dilemma is becoming apparent: If jobs are automated into oblivion, wages will also become extinct. How then do families, Catholic or otherwise maintain purchasing power, drive demand and sustain economic growth and vitality? Machines do not purchase the products they make, if wages become so low that purchasing power is lost, how is it possible for our free market economy to survive? Additionally, loss of purchasing power means humans go without: they don't go to restaurants, visit doctors or dentists, they don't join clubs or groups, apply for mortgages or operate pay TV, nor do they turn up to Church or put money in the plate!

The National Australia Bank has identified that 50% of Australians are living from payday to payday, unable to pay for emergency costs and expect to have around $150K superannuation in retirement. Such statistics underline a potential poverty crisis for half the Australian population. Current estimates suggest over $1M is needed in superannuation for adequate retirement income. The greatest problem facing Australia at the moment is not refugees, Aboriginal issues or climate change, it is employment. The Australian Catholic Church needs to embrace this reality quickly.

In 1963 American President John F. Kennedy noted a problem with the American economy. The economy needed to create thousands of new jobs each month just to keep pace with population growth. Kennedy recognised that "we have a combination of older workers who have been thrown out of work because of technology and younger people coming in with the little education". This mirrors the difficulties in the Australian workplace in 2017.

The most widespread and accepted solution to workforce stress, in both older and younger workers, is a greater emphasis on retraining and increasing technical skills. This works well in theory, yet the on-the-ground reality is vastly different. Most universities and high educational institutions report little improvement in high school standards and technical and further educational institutions produce thousands of graduates still unprepared and under-skilled for work. It appears Australia has reached a limit both in the educational capabilities of many young people already undertaking constant courses along with extreme competition for smaller number of highly skilled and well paid roles. The truth appears to be, that we are unable to upgrade the large percentage of the workforce still engaged in relatively routine and repetitive work. This cohort of both older and younger workers under increasing threat from automation and lower wages must be a primary concern and responsibility of Australia Catholicism.

In recent years, there has arisen a view which suggest that automation and reliance on technology is hampering humanity in other ways. This view suggests that the internet generation and improved technologies, in GPS, and computing is actually impacting on our ability to think and problem solve. Are we less able to apply basic logic to find our way home without the aid of the GPS. Apparently we are.

No doubt, the impact on people from increasing automation and robotics will continue to be wide and varied, but it seems highly unlikely that it can be stopped or slowed in any way. The significant levels of wealth, comfort and increased life span are all directly related to the continued development of technology. The question for Catholicism is how do we maintain our central focus on humanity, particularly if lower educated and older Australians are to be denied the basic experience of dignity proffered though the world of work.

In recent years another radical idea has been suggested. This idea is grounded in a basic income guarantee to be provided by Western governments to each citizen. This payment to all would act as a minimal safety net and not impact on any other income that may be received through employment. The theory sees this payment as an incentive for some to continue to improve their education and work potential without the fear of long-term unemployment. The praxis of providing a universal safety net without creating a disincentive to work, would require enough finance to get by without making this too comfortable.

The Catholic Church needs to consider its response to this theory and no doubt the many others that will be suggested in future years. Should the Church be happy about increasing every person's dependence on government for support? What happens to those who decide not to participate in work? Will these individuals be viewed as somehow less valuable or will there be greater social or health impacts on their lives? In a more dystopian view, will we be creating individuals who do little else but consume alcohol or drugs or who turn to crime. It is vital that the Catholic Church promotes a view of humanity that is beyond labelling any person unproductive or useless. Humanity, made in the image of God does not have such an option, but it is only the Catholic Church which is, specifically called to reflect such a position. Would the Catholic Church in Australia be happy to see Australians within a two tier system, where some never work, and others enjoy substantial benefits gifted from their ability to work?

Australian Catholics need to begin now a consideration of what the future world of work looks like. Without such an elaboration of a Catholic interpretation of human work and value, the Church not only deems itself irrelevant to this important discussion, but ensures that a future without our voice may harm the humanity of many Australians.

XIX

BE YOURSELF: CONTENDING WITH BIO-ENHANCED SOCIETY

Australians have always shown a keen fondness for adopting new technologies, whether it be mobile phones, smart TV's, smart watches, drones or our long-standing love for the car, although these now come with heads-up displays and GPS's. Most of these new inventions have entered our daily lives without any significant discussion or forethought. If something is newer, faster, better Australians appear irresistibly drawn to its implementation.

Unsurprisingly, we have also been at the forefront of acceptance for technology that promises improvement to ourselves. Nose surgery, breast enlargement, laser eye surgery, facelifts, have all become common-place in Australian society. Many of these surgeries are now regarded as entirely reasonable avenues of self-improvement, self-confidence and self-fulfilment.

Additionally, our constant search for improvement and enhancement sees Australians spearheading the world in pharmaceutical uptake. The variety of drugs available and the huge numbers of Australians taking these drugs gives rise to a new phenomenon in Australia. The "medicalisation" of many physical and mental conditions has removed the necessity of personal responsibility.

Australians now use a wide variety of drugs for, anxiety, depression and stress. These drugs promise the possibility of better lives, better relationships, a happier and healthier humanity, although we do know that not all of these drugs are successful and that not all work in the ways intended. There is still little discussion on the wider usage of drugs in our society and little understanding of drug taking beyond the alleviation of psychological symptoms. Is drug taking to temporarily remove boredom or drudgery in life a valid use? The number of individuals charged with violent assaults whilst under the influence of drugs is another area we have not explored. The Catholic Church has said nothing on any of these matters and our silence again leaves faithful Catholics without the resources to make decisions on these questions. We are in Australia, at the gateway of a multitude of new possibilities and technology for the enhancement of human beings. Our clear tendency in Australia is to enter these developments without any thought or consideration.

For example, those families who live with Down syndrome children judge them to be amongst the happiest and joyful children in the world. Yet, a number of Western nations brutally have succeeded in eradicating most pre-born Down syndrome babies. Iceland is the first nation to pride itself on the total destruction of in-utero Down syndrome children. In Iceland, 100% of all these diagnosed with Down syndrome are aborted. The United States is close to these abortion rates, now ensuring 90% of such babies are aborted. The advent of a new blood test for Down syndrome has contributed to these higher abortion rates, but overwhelmingly the most decisive factor is the content of medical advice to parents which in decisive ways suggests Down syndrome children cannot be active members of society, have cognitive disabilities which prevent meaningful employment and require lifetime care. Such medical advice is largely false, but more importantly what discussion in relation to Down syndrome children has occurred in any nation, including Australia? Why are such actions unknown to the general population and why is this not an issue for Australian Catholics given our central value on the right to life? We cannot always assume that medical experts will hold similar values to our own, but it is central that we consider these questions in our faith life and parish witness.

The Catholic Church is under sustained challenge from emerging technologies but more significantly from emerging philosophies, all of which seek to contest and ultimately supplant the broad "spirit of life" found in Catholic ethics and philosophy.

Recently, Geelong Grammar School, of which I am a former chaplain, has sidelined the teaching of the faith by the introduction of "positive psychology", a program to be taught across the whole school and integrated into all classroom subjects. Such a philosophy and program appears optimistic in its outward appearance, but leaves some significant questions and dilemmas unanswered. The philosophy seeks to identify and enhance the key factors in human flourishing and how they might be encouraged and strengthened in the schools' students. A broad list includes, security, dignity, autonomy, personal fulfilment, authenticity, fairness, interpersonal connectedness, civil engagement and transcendence.

Naturally, the church has significant things to say on these issues as well, but in a radically different way. For Catholics, personal fulfilment is not to be found exclusively in creativity or intellectual exploration. Fulfilment is found most clearly in service for it is only in service that we fully understand the human condition. Authenticity is another dimension of positive psychology that leads to a "thine own self be true philosophy". Catholics would argue that many individuals have been ruined by pursuit of happiness that only puts ourselves first. Catholicism has a definitive answer to "what is my inner nature, - we are only brought to completion in the person of Christ and in following him". For Catholics, human dignity is also a call to an array of inalienable rights, yet we also recognise that the freedom of rights must be under the freedom of self-restraint, the freedom of love of neighbour (even if that requires tough responses) and the freedom to love fully, which always requires placing others first.

Most modern philosophies are no different from the ancient ones. They seek to place humanity, our happiness and our goals at the centre of our psychology. The Church has always called for a deeper understanding, Catholicism must speak out in opposition to such positive, but ultimately, self-energised philosophies and our Catholic faithful need to hear much more of why the Church finds these philosophies ultimately unfulfilling and sometimes self-destructive.

New bio-enhancement technologies seek to grant humans new measures of control over their own lives and the natural world. Such a view proposes that the chief human quality is one of promethean restlessness which seeks control of our own evolutionary process, according to our values and free of constraints. This process is thought to achieve new levels of happiness, creativity and achievement.

A philosophy which says pursuing our own potential is what gives our lives meaning, will always result in the elimination of Down syndrome babies, or whatever the next human imperfections are thought to be. Australian Catholics need a vigorous voice in again arguing for service and vocation as central human values.

XX

THE CATHOLIC CASE FOR LOWER TAXES

—with Aaron Lane

Lower rates of tax increase disposable incomes, and increase the ability of a family to provide for itself.

Families are the principal units in society, not the state. The Catechism of the Catholic Church teaches that "the family is the original cell of social life" and "the family must be helped and defended by appropriate social measures" which involves "the right to private property, to free enterprise, to obtain work and housing" (*Catechism of the Catholic Church*, nn. 2207-2213). Taxation rates above those that are necessary to provide for the fundamental roles of government (i.e. defence, law and order) mean that politicians' and bureaucrats' plans are preferred over individual's plans. The best welfare system is a strong family unit. The principle of subsidiarity suggests that taxes should be as low as possible to allow families to provide for themselves. Lower taxes, and higher disposable incomes, allow families to save – and this is particularly for young families trying to enter the property market.

On income tax, attention should be paid to marginal tax rates. In addition to the reasons outlined above, high marginal tax rates may force both parents to work where this might be contrary to living out their true vocation. Other current priorities include taxes on property that will increase rents and reduce housing prices – and taxes on superannuation which will impact older Australians approaching retirement, and limit their ability to be self-sufficient.

High taxes can make everybody poorer.

We noted in the previous section that Catholic principles dictate a tax system must be based on "justice and equity". A system which makes everybody poorer cannot be just, or equitable – and simply cannot be tolerated. There is a trade-off between the tax rate and the tax revenue – illustrated by the Laffer curve, below. The central idea is that there is a maximum amount of revenue that a government can collect. Its usefulness in this discussion is that if the marginal tax rate is already high (in order to redistribute income, or provide high levels of government services), then future hikes in the tax rate will actually reduce government revenues. This is in no-way 'trickle-down economics' – but recognises that incentives are powerful.

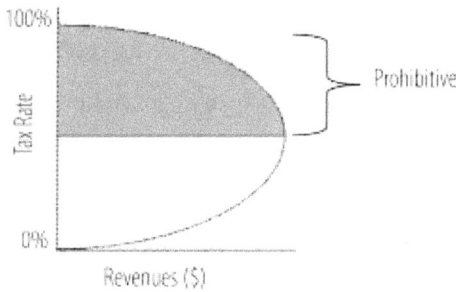

The Laffer curve

Higher Taxes reduce the incentive for people to work, while lower tax rates foster the ability of businesses to employ people.

There is dignity in work – and, for those able, a moral duty. As St. John Paul II teaches, "Man must work out of regard for others, especially his own family, but also for the society he belongs to, the country of which he is a child, and the whole human family of which he is a member, since he is the heir to the work of generations and at the same time a sharer in building the future of those who will come after him in the succession of history. All this constitutes the moral obligation of work..." (*Laborem Exercens*, n. 16).

Economic theory dictates that higher rates of income tax will reduce effort and production – which create individual and collective wealth. Work should be encouraged, and measures to reduce the tax burden on individuals should be supported. Likewise, company tax – and other specific business taxes such as payroll tax – will influence employment and employment growth. According to the Australian Chamber of Commerce and Industry, there are over two million small businesses in Australia which employ over seven million people – accounting for over 60 per of the Australian workforce. With crippling rates of youth unemployment in some pockets of the country, and many older workers facing structural unemployment in older manufacturing industries, policies to stimulate employment growth are of vital importance.

Behavioural taxation can have perverse consequences, and hurt the poor.

The Australian tax system features a range of excise taxes, such as those levied on alcohol and tobacco. Under the banner of 'preventative health', governments justify tax hikes to reduce consumers' consumption of products that might have negative health consequences.

However, there are two moral issues that need to be considered where governments propose to increase these taxes even further. First, research from Deakin University (Miller & Droste, 2013) found that if taxes increase sufficiently on alcoholic products, consumers will substitute for illegal drugs– making matters even worse. Similarly, there are reports that link increased taxes on tobacco to increased consumption of illegal tobacco. Second, it is well-known that people with lower incomes are much more likely to smoke (see: National Drug Strategy Household Survey, 2013) – which means that the poorest will be the hardest hit by regressive tax increases.

Tax is not a substitute for charitable giving

The Church has faithfully taught that people should give to others that which they do not need for themselves. Increased taxation reduces the ability – and importantly, reduces the perceived obligation – for charitable giving (although it is noted tax deductibility goes some way to mitigate these effects). While there is arguably a role for a level of taxation to fund government programs for those that cannot provide for themselves (e.g. disabled, elderly, unemployed, etc.) – policy makers must be careful that government programs do not crowd out private acts of charity.

As Pope Benedict XVI notes, "We do not need a state which regulates and controls everything, but a State which, in accordance with the principle of subsidiarity, generously acknowledges and supports initiatives arising from the different social forces and combines spontaneity with closeness to those in need" (Benedict XVI, *Deus Caritas Est,* n. 28).

THE BATTLE FOR AUSTRALIAN CATHOLICISM

www.ingramcontent.com/pod-product-compliance
Lightning Source LLC
Chambersburg PA
CBHW071847230426
43671CB00012B/2095